NEW YEATS PAPERS I

THE YEATS FAMILY AND THE POLLEXFENS OF SLIGO BY WILLIAM M. MURPHY WITH DRAWINGS BY JOHN BUTLER YEATS

THE DOLMEN PRESS

CONTENTS

General Editor : Liam Miller

This paper is a development of a lecture delivered to the Yeats International Summer School at Sligo, on 15 August, 1968.

Printed and published in the Republic of Ireland at the Dolmen Press, 8 Herbert Place, Dublin 2. First published in 1971. Distributed outside Ireland, except in the United States of America and in Canada, by Oxford University Press.

To
the memory of
JEANNE ROBERT FOSTER
(1879 - 1970)

who, if not the onlie begetter of these ensuing pages,
was the first and the dearest.

JOHN BUTLER YEATS (1839 - 1922), a distinguished portrait painter in his own right, had good reason to be proud of his equally talented children. His older son, William Butler Yeats (1865 - 1939), was a Nobel Laureate in Literature, and his younger, John Butler Yeats, Jr. ('Jack') (1871 - 1957), was a great painter whose reputation grows yearly. His two daughters were women of exceptional talents : Susan Mary ('Lily') (1866 - 1949), an artist of embroidery, was also a woman of wide ranging interests and the possessor of a sharp and sensuous prose style; and Elizabeth Corbet ('Lollie') (1868 - 1940) was the publisher of the books that were issued under the imprint of the famous Cuala Press. For their many gifts he could have thanked his own ancestors, of whom he was justly proud, a mixture of folk connected with the Church of Ireland, the Dublin Castle Anglo-Irish ascendancy, and the English military. In the remoter past were Dublin merchants, French Huguenots, and Butlers of the noble Ormonde family. John Butler Yeats loved the family of his father, with its many uncles and aunts, the children of Parson John Yeats, of Drumcliff Parish near Sligo. Of his uncles Thomas and John he wrote to his daughter Lily : 'You would be proud to have their blood. They were so clever and so innocent. I never knew and never will know any people so attractive.'[1] 'They were like wild snow drops,' he said on another occasion, '— *capricious* and *gentle* and *pure*. Merely to be near them was to me a happiness.'[2] Commending his own son William Butler Yeats on the possession of some amiable quality, he claims the credit for its transmission : 'I say this remembering my father's family. They all of them in every fibre of their being were "The Good People".'[3]

Yet he was by no means sure that the remarkable qualities of his sons and daughters sprang from the amiable Yeatses. His wife, born Susan Pollexfen in Sligo, was herself an offshoot of a family of strange richness and depth. When Edward Dowden, Professor of Literature at Trinity College Dublin, wrote his old schoolfellow in January 1884 that he was impressed by some unpublished early poems that the eighteen-year old William Butler Yeats had left with him, JBY sought no honour for himself or for his own family :

I am glad you are so pleased with Willie. It is curious that long ago I was struck by finding in his mother's people all the marks of imagination, the continual absorption in an idea — and that idea never one of the intellectual and reasoning faculty but of the affections and desires and the senses.[4]

While Susan Pollexfen Yeats herself may have contributed little to the character of her children and almost nothing to their intellectual development, the family of which she was a member exercised, far more than the Yeatses, a profound influence on her four children; and their father, who saw in them the marks of his wife's family, continually reminded them of the twin streams that fed the river of their genius. He was endlessly fascinated by his wife's family, and his running analysis of it constitutes much of the subject matter of his letters to his children. He never allowed them to forget their double heritage. Possessing his own articulateness and, at times, his bubbling enthusiasm, they could not shake off the

8

intensity, the solemnity, the tendency to melancholia of their mother's family, which stuck to them like burrs.

In analysing his children their father continually made use of his favourite comparison, whether the purpose was serious or frivolous. In 1911 Lollie Yeats, suffering from nervous exhaustion, had undertaken a tour to Italy to soothe her nerves. John Butler Yeats wrote to his brother Isaac of a letter he had received from her. It was

full of bitter delusions about everybody. It was quite crazy, and I came to the conclusion that her trip had not done her good but on the contrary made her worse. There are in her two races, the Yeats and the Pollexfen. Sometimes she is one and sometimes the other. When she is Yeats she is happy and making the best of things. When she is Pollexfen she makes the worst of things. . . . [She has] the Pollexfen tendency to be morbid and unhappy.[5]

On another occasion, when JBY in New York received an unexpected large gift of money from his son the poet he delightedly wrote his older daughter Lily:

. . . it may be endlessly debated whether Willie is a Pollexfen or a Yeats. The fact is he is both, one side of him not one bit like a Pollexfen, and another side not a bit like a Yeats. It was like a Yeats to send this money and make no fuss about it. It was like a Pollexfen to have it to send.[6]

The weaving of the complex tapestry of the Yeats children began at the Atholl Academy on the Isle of Man in the early 1850's. There a group of Irish and English boys underwent the penitential and purgatorial schooling under a flogging Scottish schoolmaster that was the standard of private educa-

9

tion in those days. Three of the Irish boys were the Yeats brothers from County Down, John Butler, William Butler, and Robert Corbet;[7] two others were the Pollexfen brothers from Sligo, Charles, the elder, and his brother George, born in the same year as Johnnie Yeats, 1839. Although they had not met before, the five boys all had connections with Sligo. The Yeats grandfather, John, had been Rector of Drumcliff from 1811 to 1846 and was long active in the political affairs of the town of Sligo. His children Matthew, Thomas, and Mary ('Aunt Mickey') remained in the area for a long time after his death. Matthew, a land agent, was involved in the 'striping' of the Rosses in 1860;[8] Uncle Thomas, a learned mathematician and a sweet and humane man, abandoned a promising career to help support 'Mickey' (1821 - 1891), a delightful maiden lady who lived on the outskirts of the town, and their Aunt Charlotte (1792 - 1872), also unmarried.[9]

The Pollexfen boys came from a different kind of family altogether. They were the oldest of eleven children — two others died young — of a transplanted Englishman of Devonshire birth and Cornish ancestry. William Pollexfen, born 1811, was descended from a younger branch of the family that then occupied — and still occupies — Kitley Manor in Yealmpton, Devon. Born at Berry Head, near the port of Brixham, he had run away to sea at twelve years of age. While still in his early twenties he found himself in Sligo where his cousin Elizabeth Pollexfen Middleton, a Jersey girl, was a widow whose husband William, a Sligo man of the merchant firm of Middleton and Mills, had died in the cholera epidemic of 1832 that had almost wiped out Sligo. After several visits

William Pollexfen decided to remain. He married his cousin's daughter, also named Elizabeth, eight years his junior, and entered into a partnership with her brother, also named William, under the firm name of Middleton and Pollexfen. They owned ships that imported coal to and maize from America and carried goods from Sligo and Liverpool to Portugal and Spain.[10] In nearby Ballysodare, a mill town from prehistoric times, Robert Culberson had built in the 1830's an oatmeal mill on the right bank of the river and a flour mill on the left. A terrible explosion in 1856 killed nine people and maimed many others and led to the untimely death from grief of Mr. Culberson. Middleton and Pollexfen bought up the property and on the business generated from it established a considerable family fortune.[11] In the early 50's, however, when the boys were at school, William Pollexfen was merely a rising but not yet wealthy merchant, completely devoted to business and not interested in providing for more than the barest education for his children, who were expected if they were boys to make their way in the world of business and if they were girls to marry well.

It was their Irishness and Sligo associations that brought the two sets of brothers together at Atholl, for there was intense rivalry between the English and the Irish. The Irish were usually at the top, despite the fact that most of them took the difficult academic preparatory programme requiring Latin and Greek while the English took the easier commercial subjects. John Butler Yeats himself always headed the class, and his younger brother Willie was the most popular and attractive boy in the school.[12]

The Pollexfens were of a different breed. Having come to the school 'badly educated' (as JBY expressed it) they always stood at the foot of the class. But they were not only poor students; they were also disagreeable as people. Both were unpopular, refusing to take part in games, although they could play well enough. George could be surly, and when the fit was on him his brother Charles 'would allow no one to approach who were not his inferiors and flatterers.' It 'hurt their pride and spoiled their tempers' to be always at the foot of the class. In their solid and brooding presence there was something forbidding. Even 'the master let them alone. They were not the sort to be interfered with.'[13]

Nevertheless George Pollexfen fascinated John Butler Yeats. He was his most 'intimate' and indeed his 'only' friend, though whether 'friend' is the correct word is perhaps a decision that analysts of their relationship would like to make for themselves. 'I don't think George took any interest in me then or at any time,' JBY wrote sixty years later in his Memoirs, 'but from the first I was greatly interested in him and never lost my interest.'[14] He came to believe, in the retrospection of old age, that it was George's melancholy that first attracted him.[15] He was 'slow and tedious in all his movements,'[16] and the headmaster 'disliked him because of his unresponsiveness.'[17] Among people whom he did not know well or felt uncomfortable with, then as all his life he was not merely unresponsive but chilly. 'Socially,' wrote his schoolfriend of him, 'he was worse than a bore, he was an iceberg. In his presence conversation grew languid and then stopped.' Yet, 'in the intimacy of personal conversation he was irresistible, also as a monologist . . . a poet who in Wordsworth's phrase had not "the sweet accomplishment of verse".[18] In the large dormitory at the school, where he slept with nine or ten other boys, he wore a face the headmaster never saw:

Night after night he would keep these boys wide awake and perfectly still while he told them stories, made impromptu as he went along. . . . He was as rich in natural fertility as a virgin forest. . . . What he knew he presented without philosophy, without theories, without ideas, in a language that recalled the vision of the early poets. . . . He talked poetry though he did not know it.[19]

In him JBY recognised something which he called 'magnetism,' and which he was to call also 'sincerity' or 'intensity' or 'primitivism,' by which he meant a closeness to nature, an almost animal connection with earth, air, and water, the stuff of which poets and poetry are made. He found such magnetism in all the Pollexfens, even in Charles, the older brother, who presented only its negative pole to those around him. He was 'openly hostile'.[20]

If you tried to be friendly with him invariably he insulted you, *and he knew all his life long how to inflict pain*. . . . Yet *he had . . . magnetism*.[21]

These lines were written in 1916 in a letter to William Butler Yeats, and to them JBY added: 'I have not seen him for 40 years and hope I may never see him.'

After Atholl John Butler Yeats went on to Trinity College Dublin, to which he tried with his father's help to entice George. But against William Pollexfen's invincible opposition to education they could make no headway. George instead was sent on one of the family steamers, 'The Bacalieu', to Portugal and Spain, and after seasoning in the Sligo offices of his father's company went to Ballina to represent the family business there.[22]

In the summer of 1862 John Butler Yeats, with a new degree from Trinity College and ten pounds in his pocket won in a prize competition in Political Economy in which he was the only entrant,[23] journeyed to Sligo to see his old school friend. The Pollexfens were staying for the summer at Rosses Point, the beautiful place a few miles north of Sligo, with broad sloping meadows, sandy beaches, and island-dotted bays. There he and George renewed their friendship on long walks, and the surroundings cast their spell upon him.

George talked endlessly. . . . The place was strange to me and very beautiful in the deepening twilight. A little way from us, and far down from where we talked, the Atlantic kept up its ceaseless tumult, foaming around the rocks called Dead Man's Point. Dublin . . . and Trinity College . . . were obliterated, and I was again with my school friend, the man self-centred and tranquil and on that evening so companionable.

Looking back on the visit years later he reflects on what did not occur to him at the time :

I have sometimes an amused curiosity in thinking whether he cared for me at all, or how much he cared, but it has been only curiosity. I was always quite content with my own liking for him.[24]

Among the Pollexfens was Susan, the attractive eldest daughter, quiet and pretty, with one blue eye and one brown

14

eye, each of unambiguous colour.[25] It was a glorious vacation, and under the spell of the place John and Susan found themselves drifting together. The courtship developed at Rosses Point and in the caves at Bundoran,[26] and just before JBY returned to Dublin to take up his studies for the bar they announced their engagement.

A short time later, on 24 November, 1862, John Butler Yeats's father died suddenly and the young man found himself the possessor of the family properties consisting of 346 acres, 2 roods, and 25 perches[27] in County Kildare and of a house in Dorset Street, Dublin. He returned to Sligo the following summer, and on 10 September, 1863, the Pollexfens watched with pride and satisfaction as their daughter was married to an authentic Irish landlord, a descendant of the Butlers and of respectable clergymen, and a bright young star in the Kings Inns of Dublin. It would surely have surprised them all to know that that was virtually the last time they would be pleased with John Butler Yeats.

At Rosses Point and Bundoran a year earlier JBY had seen the family only on summer vacation, and his own hours were spent largely in walks with George and courtship with Susan. But what he saw of the family charmed him. Bred in the happy ease of the Yeatses, he had never imagined, despite his acquaintanceship with Charles and George, that the possibilities of human existence could include anything so strange as the Pollexfens, with their morose and solid strength and their devotion to principle, a people unyielding, serious, sombre, with no time for joy or the pleasures of the intellect. 'I was fascinated', he wrote;[28] and he never lost the fascination.

15

Now in Sligo he saw the genus in its natural habitat. The family had not yet moved into the spacious quarters of Merville, the large country house at the edge of town, but lived in a small house in Union Place. At the time of the marriage the Pollexfen family had been completed. Alice, the youngest child, was six years old. There were three other daughters besides Susan: Isabella, fourteen, Elizabeth, ten, and Agnes, eight. After Charles and George came four other sons ranging in age from eighteen to nine. JBY wrote his elder son a vivid account of their Sundays at home:

. . . the family gathered in force and sat together mostly in one room, and all disliking each other, at any rate alien mutually, in gloomy silence broken only by the sound of your grandmother turning over the leaf of a book, or by the creaking of some one's brace, or by a sigh from George Pollexfen.[29]

They were a strange people, intense, silent, brooding: 'the crossest people I ever met,' Ellen Yeats laughingly said of them.[30] Yet the flame that burned within they could only feel, not see. They were poets and mystics *ex nativitate* who rejected the natural impulses their God had given them. In the family was a talent for art and music, and JBY observed that they had 'a wonderful facility in picking up and remembering anything in the papers written in rhyme', yet they 'despised literature and poetry as being part of that idleness which they regarded as so calamitous to morals.'[31] The combination was charged with lightning. If they had been Yeatses only, JBY's children might have become something quite different, something blander; but as Pollexfens too they were blessed with

16

what their father later came to consider the perfect mixture of fuel and fire.[32]

The Pollexfens were as solid and powerful as the sea-cliffs; 'but hitherto they are altogether dumb', JBY wrote Dowden. 'To give them a voice is like giving a voice to the sea-cliffs, when what wild babblings must break forth.'[33] Through his son William Butler Yeats JBY gave a tongue to the sea-cliffs.

For the Pollexfen influence on his children JBY himself was largely responsible, as he failed to overcome the defects in his own character that might have kept him fully in control of his own and his family's destiny. He returned with his bride to Dublin to continue his studies in the law, and by 1866 two children, William Butler and Susan Mary, had been born. Then his promising career took a sharp turn. The young barrister had become increasingly discontented with the prospect of a long life in the Four Courts. In college he had been deeply influenced by the philosophical probings of people like John Todhunter and the Dowden brothers, John and Edward, who lived the life of the mind and were interested in first principles. He had rejected Christianity, been converted by Darwin, and was on his way to becoming a Comtist. To his intellectual bent was added a talent for drawing. At school he had sketched his fellow pupils and even the masters; now he lightened irksome hours in court by sketching judges and counsel, sometimes in wicked caricature.[34] As the Law came to look duller and duller he found himself increasingly more curious about the theory of art and its place in the universe of values. In early 1867, in the face of the open hostility of his wife's family and the horrified apprehension of his own, he aban-

17

doned Dublin and the Law and settled in London to begin, at the age of twenty-eight, the long and arduous training of the artist. The results, as the world well knows, were in the short run disastrous. JBY proved a perfectionist who could never finish a picture ('You had to look for the crucial moment and snatch it from the easel when you thought it was right,' Mr. C. P. Curran has said).[35] To his impracticality as an artist he added an incapacity for business and finance. Unhappily, the family properties in Kildare were heavily encumbered and yielded barely enough to keep their owner above insolvency, yet for years they were virtually his sole source of income. The result was that Susan Yeats's father had to help support the family, Susan became increasingly more discontented and querulous, and she and the children, who by 1871 included 'Lollie', Robert Corbet ('Bobbie', who died in 1873 when not quite three), and 'Jack', found themselves living for long periods of time at the home of her parents in Sligo while the father struggled alone in London.

So although the overmastering personality of JBY left the deepest impression on all the Yeats children,[36] it is not surprising that that of the Pollexfens followed close behind. Aunt 'Mickey' and JBY's Uncle Matthew still lived in Sligo — Thomas Yeats had died when the children were young — but their nephews and nieces saw little of them.[37] A few times when young they visited Grandmother Yeats at her house at 47 Leeson Street in Dublin, but she died in 1876, and thereafter the children were seldom in Dublin until they returned to live there in 1881, when Willie was sixteen.

By that time their souls had been shaped, and it was Sligo

18

that shaped them, the beautiful little town lying almost at the western tip of Europe, its narrow streets lined by small shops, its margins green fields, mountains, and the sea. The children loved Sligo as they hated London. In that giant city were no relatives of any kind, and outside were only the roadway and the pavements grey. At Sligo there were the ships loading and unloading, the sight of Ben Bulben and Knocknarea, the stoning of raisins for the Christmas pudding, the Hazelwood Racecourse with 'the crowds, the smell of bruised grass, the thud of the horses over the jumps.' In London the servants could talk of nothing but murders and suicides. In Sligo, said Lily, 'The servants played a big part in our lives. They were so friendly and wise and knew so intimately angels, saints, banshees, and fairies.'[38] For years as adults the Yeats offspring returned there whenever they could. Lily annually spent her vacation there. When she worked at embroidery for May Morris in London from 1888 to 1894 she took an extra week off without pay every year and travelled by night both ways to get as much time as possible in Sligo.[39] It was the real home of Jack Yeats during his most impressionable years, when he lived there with his grandfather and grandmother, and the spiritual home to which his older brother often returned and from which he was much more often exiled.[40] And that home was peopled not by Yeatses but by Pollexfens.

As John Butler Yeats came to know the Pollexfens better he saw in them three qualities he would have preferred them not to possess, with only their magnetism and suppressed poetry to counteract them. The three were a striving for property, a worship of class, and an unhappy tendency to depressive melancholia. The third of these perhaps could not be helped; the first two grew out of the misguided views of old William Pollexfen. His grandson was to extol him as the 'silent and fierce old man', but the description hardly suggests his complex nature. He had run away to sea as a boy, lived the hard life of a sailor, and performed feats of derring-do of which he never spoke and which his family learned of, sometimes years later, only from the mouths of others. He would not ask his men on the Sligo steamers to do anything he would not do himself and once dived beneath a ship in Sligo harbour to see what was wrong with the rudder when the men refused his command to go down. Having no education himself he saw no need for it in others. He kept on the wall of his bedroom a painting of the ancestral home, Kitley Manor, and may have seen himself as the founding father of a new dynasty. He admired spirit and courage and resourcefulness and despised people, including his own sons, who were deficient in them. 'Only the wasteful virtues earn the sun', was the lesson his oldest grandchild learned from him — though of course he scarcely admired those who wandered in the moonshine, as WBY's father seemed to him to be doing. Gruff and cross, he terrorised and impressed his grandchildren merely by the power of his presence. When WBY thought of him in later years the figure of King Lear rose before him.[41] Lily, something of a Cordelia, saw him differently:

Grandpapa Pollexfen we liked, admired, and avoided. He never talked to anyone. He grumbled, complained, and ejaculated all day long. The past and the future had no interest for him at all. He was in such a state of irritation with the present moment that he could think of nothing else. He was quite unsuspicious so it was only what he saw that irritated, so there was everything to be said for 'keeping out of the master's way'. We grandchildren did it, only seeing him at meals, and then sitting if possible on the same side of the table so that he could not be driven mad by seeing us take too much sugar. He had an alarming way of stopping grumbling and eating and looking at us in silence while we carried two sugar spoons from the bowl to our plates.[42]

He was a man of direct action. Lily writes that the tapping of the top of a boiled egg infuriated him. 'His way,' Lily writes, 'was to hold the egg cup firmly on its plate with his left hand, then with a sharp knife in his right hand to behead the egg with one blow. Where the top of the egg went to was not his business. It might hit a grandchild or the ceiling. He never looked.'

A French girl visiting one of the Pollexfen daughters heard him say he did not mind loud noises, only soft ones. She 'stooped and, picking up all the fire irons, flung them all from the height of the mantelpiece crashing into the fender. There was an awful pause. No one spoke. Grandpapa went slowly out of the room and to bed.' His impatience could also be aroused by lemonade bottles:

In those days the bottles were corked and wired. You took off the wire and gently moved the cork from side to side and out it came. Grandpapa took off the wire, gave the cork a few violent side to side shakes, then shook the bottle till the lemonade bubbled and foamed up, then he held the bottle at arm's length and out blew the cork and most of the lemonade.[43]

Since his interest was only in business he wasted no time on the spiritual upbringing or social training of his children. The difference between life in the Yeats and Pollexfen households struck Lily. At Grandmama's house in Leeson Street, she wrote,

I was never so happy before. Grandmama Yeats was demonstrative, called me pet names, caressed me. I followed her about. She gave me feathers to stuff a doll's mattress, got them then and there from the cook plucking a chicken. I was put to bed by several merry aunts. They all ran about, laughed, played. Grandmama Yeats had nicknames and pet names for things as well as grandchildren. Her scissors had a name. The house was full of old things. Everything in the house had a story.

The Pollexfen grandparents' house — all was serious, silent. There was no merry talk there. People walked soberly about. There were no pet names or caresses. Life was serious and silent, no merry talk at meals, no running to and fro.[44]

His wife was the only person who could manage William Pollexfen. She was kind and charitable, a lady by right divine, as her son-in-law was to acknowledge. Lily wrote of her:

She had a tranquillizing effect on all, but most of all on him. She smoothed all the wrinkles out of his life she could. Such little things as collar pins he was too impatient to manage, so she every week sewed little black silk ties on to his week's supply of shirts and so got rid of one irritation. Sometimes when he was worse than usual she would look nervous and blink her eyes. He would look at her, give a short laugh, and be quiet.[45]

She was a calm and even-tempered person who had been born

22

into a comfortable world and appreciated her good fortune. Her mother, Elizabeth Pollexfen Middleton, was the daughter of the Rev. Charles Pollexfen of Jersey, where she had been discovered, courted, and married by William Middleton of Sligo, a partner in the ship-owning firm of Middleton and Mills. He was a widower of forty-three with no children when he married his fifteen-year old bride. Dying in the cholera epidemic of 1832, he left his widow with several children, among them William, who was to take over the family business, and the youngest daughter Elizabeth, born in 1819. It was the widow's cousin William Pollexfen who sailed into Sligo on his own ship, 'The Dasher', to offer a helping hand, married the daughter in 1837, and stayed in Sligo for the rest of his life, joining with his wife's brother William in the new firm of Middleton and Pollexfen.[46]

Elizabeth Middleton Pollexfen had been born in a house in Wine Street, Sligo. She attended Sligo's only school and studied painting and music at the Convent. After her marriage she and her husband lived in the Wine Street house with her mother. There were servants to take care of the heavy work, and as children came along Mrs. Middleton more and more managed things. So the life of the young mother was an easy one, and she grew apologetic when telling her granddaughter Lily Yeats about it. She was known and liked throughout the village for her kindness and good works, and the nuns at the Convent remembered their old friendship with her by asking her from time to time for flowers and subscriptions.

They remained in the Wine Street house until 1845, when the growing family moved to Union Place, where Grandmother Middleton died in 1853, by which time all but three of the Pollexfen children who were to survive childhood had been born. All the while the family fortunes were improving. By 1867, when JBY took off for London, the Pollexfens were prosperous enough to leave Union Place for Merville, the big house on 60 acres of land at the edge of town with its magnificent view of Ben Bulben, and in that year William Middleton had enough spare capital to purchase from the Misses Cooper the entire area of The Rosses, for which he paid £17,500 and on which he was soon to spend an additional £2,500 for improvements.[47]

Over the big household Elizabeth Pollexfen presided with grace and dignity. Although there were many maids she never had servant trouble. She was kind and sympathetic to the many young girls who came and went, always remembered them on their birthdays, and wrote regularly to those who emigrated to America. Every day, clothed simply but correctly —'black silk dress, real lace cap, collar and cuffs, quilted black satin petticoat, thin cream-coloured stockings, and thin black shoes'— she drove about in the outside car or the phaeton and 'looked about her all the time for people to whom she could give a gift'.[48] She was the perfect lady, calm, ordered, generous, sensible.

But if she appealed to her grandchildren by her kindness and gentleness, she apparently had little influence on the upbringing of her sons who, in the finest Victorian tradition, were the responsibility of their father. He let them know the kind of goal he wished them to aspire to and then left them to shift for themselves. It was he who inculcated in them

24

those false values which his first son-in-law so vainly deplored. Among the Pollexfens, JBY wrote to WBY years later, there was 'a very strong sense of property'. 'Their canons did not permit them to indulge in an affection for their children, so they clung the more to houses and lands.'[49] In JBY's view it was a tragedy, for he thought their devotion to money a matter of principle only, not love. It was the right and proper thing to worship, but it went against their natures. They were 'primitives,' full of 'sovereign human nature, so shy and scared with its heroic heart, its strange isolation, and its strange unselfishness, and its inability to explain itself or indeed do anything except be itself.'[50]

Unfortunately something had happened to them. A destructive form of puritanism had warped their values, given them false gods to worship, and caused them to suppress all that was finest and best in themselves. Perhaps the source of the evil could be found in William Pollexfen's background and his own special place in Ireland. He had brought with him from England a consciousness of landed distinction in his ancestry, reinforced by the perpetual presence on his wall of the picture of Kitley Manor. Yet as a merchant and a man of the sea he shared those economic and social values that increased the bank-accounts while they destroyed the spirit of the class-conscious merchants of England. Under the force of William Pollexfen, his family, as Professor A. N. Jeffares has pointed out, was 'orientated toward England' because of their 'descent, religion, education, and traditions'.[51] They looked down on their Middleton relatives who, like the Yeatses, were a comfortably established old Irish family who had drifted with satisfaction into the easy ways of the people who surrounded them. But if the Pollexfens were not of a secure mercantile family like the Middletons, neither were they of an old ascendancy family like the Gore-Booths, whom they did not meet socially, nor were they of the Castle or the cathedral. They had not come to Ireland as enforcers or beneficiaries of the imperial domination but as accidental immigrants busy with trade. In their views on life and living they were more reminiscent of the Belfast Protestantism with which they had no connection than of the Church of Ireland to which they belonged.

All religions have their symbols, and in all is a tendency to confuse the symbols with the things they stand for and so create false gods. The ikon of the Puritans was money, and the Pollexfens, said JBY, thought money 'the finest and most serious thing in the world'; yet it did not penetrate their vitals. It merely 'oppressed them, turning them away from the natural ways.'[52] They did not even know what to do with it. George Pollexfen, charged his brother-in-law, enjoyed his money 'by looking at it'.[53]

With their uncritical admiration for money went their feeling for class: one had to believe oneself better than other people. It was a family blight in the Pollexfens that worried John Butler Yeats, as he was afraid it might infect his own children. He had strong opinions on the subject. 'Class feeling', he wrote Lily, 'destroys life. Because of it everyone . . . is ashamed to be their real selves, always pretending to like people and things they don't really like, and to dislike people and things they naturally would like.'[54] He called it 'a curse, a sort of imprisonment corrupting the people who benefit by it, and enraging and brutalising the others.'[55] Further, he added penetratingly, 'It is of commercial origin but apes the ways of aristocracy.'[56] Let a peasant procure more wealth than his neighbours and he wants to set himself up for a duke. True nobility was something quite different, and all his life JBY impressed upon his son the poet the necessity of membership in that other aristocracy — the fellowship of solitary artists and intellectuals. It might in the real world find itself by chance in a Coole Park and might more easily meet hospitality in such a stately mansion than in a thatched cottage. But it was the aristocracy that counted, not the roof that sheltered it. The Pollexfens had confused one thing for another and in reaching for the symbol had lost the truth. They were a natural nobility just as they were. They were aristocrats as they were poets. They should have left well enough alone.

Those familiar with William Butler Yeats's *Autobiographies*, his poems (particularly 'Pardon, Old Fathers' and *In Memory of Alfred Pollexfen*), the standard works of Hone, Jeffares, and Ellmann, Wade's edition of the Letters, and Hone's selection of JBY's letters,[57] can readily identify several Pollexfens. Perhaps Grandfather William and Uncle George stand forth most vividly. Others take vague shapes, especially as WBY often alluded to some without naming them (as he did William the younger in the *Autobiographies*), or named without precisely identifying (as he did John in *In Memory of Alfred Pollexfen*).

27

It is impossible to get a complete picture of the Pollexfens from WBY's published works and difficult to extract one from the little evidence he gives us, since, in the opinion of his father, he romanticised them beyond recognition. 'In Willie's eyes', he wrote Lily, 'they appear something grand like the figures at Stonehenge seen by moon-light.'[58] When WBY was writing of his childhood the facts had faded into impressions; he could not remember as sharply as his father the harshness of his aunts in undertaking his early education, which caused JBY to whisk him off to London, where he himself could over-see his son's intellectual development.[59] The result was WBY's own indefinite conclusion about his childhood among the Pollexfens: they 'came and went, and almost all they said or did has faded from my memory, except a few harsh words that convince me by a vividness out of proportion to their harshness that all were habitually kind and considerate.'[60]

These are kindly words and no doubt sincere. Yet they may conceal as much as they reveal. WBY was of course often indefinite by nature, but sometimes his vagueness cloaked matters he did not care to have exposed.[61] The Pollexfen aunts and uncles, as well as Grandfather William and Grandmother Elizabeth, made up a large part of the total environment of the Yeats children, and until Alfred Pollexfen's death in 1916 the association between the families was continuous and close, closer even than *Autobiographies* suggests. In varying degrees each of the Pollexfens exerted a direct or indirect influence on the Yeats children that helped to mould them into what they became.

Fortunately Charles William, the eldest (1838 - 1923), was

seldom in Sligo when the Yeats children were small, for his influence on the young was bad. JBY thought him chiefly responsible for the behaviour of the unfortunate Fredrick Pollexfen, a brother fourteen years his junior, whom he raised up in the dubious pleasures of gambling: 'the evil brother Charles', JBY called him.[62] He was a sour and unpleasant person whose opposition to JBY, beginning in their school days, sprang from a cynicism that stood in contrast to JBY's idealism and continued throughout a long life. A year before JBY married Charles's sister he wrote to his fiancée of his pleasure at hearing good news about Charles's career. 'I would send him my congratulations and good wishes,' he added, 'only he'd say it was "humbug".'[63] When Charles Pollexfen joined the marines as a young man he had to enter as a private rather than an officer because he could not work for others except under rigid discipline.[64] JBY, who wrote and received many letters during his lifetime, said the 'haughtiest letter' he ever read was from Charles Pollexfen.[65] Yet he had 'magnetism', and JBY felt its force in Charles as in George. He 'would insult me,' JBY wrote to Willie, 'while all the time I had only one idea, my admiration' for his 'force and specific weight.'[66] If only the magnetism had not been neutralised by notions of class and threaded with Puritan hatred, even he might have amounted to something. For in him there were fine qualities —'capacity for action, courage, self-reliance, and *benevolence.*' His mother told JBY about his sending an easy chair he owned to an old man he hardly knew but who needed it. Yet he drove people away, 'as he was apt to be very insulting, and could endure nobody except abject slaves and flatterers.'

29

He never recovered from his sour Puritanical upbringing and so remained 'a great fragment of human quartz'.[67]

There was not enough room in the Sligo firm for all the Pollexfen sons. But William Pollexfen and William Middleton also owned the Sligo Steam Navigation Company, which registered more than twenty-five vessels during its long history, and Charles was dispatched to manage the company's office at Liverpool, where he resided the rest of his life.[68]

Joining him there as a young man was the youngest of the Pollexfen sons, Alfred Edward (1854 - 1916), the 'stout and humourous'[69] uncle who was the most engaging and likeable of the lot, though apparently without force enough to free himself from fraternal and familial domination. A bachelor, he worked for long years in a small room under a feeble light. In him JBY found a frustrated poet, a man of natural affection not quite submerged in the man of commercial values, for which Alfred had no real respect. As a child he had cried when given a new hat and demanded the return of the old one, in which JBY saw 'the stirring of affection'.[70] He loved music; when a band came to Sligo the young boy Alfred would follow it about and remain with it until someone came to bring him home. Yet when he learned a tune he instantly mimicked it as if to pretend that it had no value. 'He made derision of his own susceptibilities', charged JBY. He played the concertina and might have become a good musician. He had no gift for business but did not know it, and the family refused to recognize it: 'It was as if a Spartan suspected one of the family of being a coward.'[71] His humour was his one gift, a rare one in the family, and he had a 'curious crooked smile' which he shared with his father and his brother Fredrick.[72] He had 'no intellect or not enough to speak about'[73] and was impervious to reason. As he could not generalize he could not judge but accepted everything as it came, and so remained cheerful and contented, a quiet drudge in the office of his domineering older brother.[74] JBY wrote to Lily:

. . . he was an extremely modest man, and very docile, so that he always accepted the world's estimate as to who was superior, who inferior. He paid respect where the world paid respect, and not because he expected to get anything by it. . . . His joys were a little pallid, like weak tea.[75]

But his real nature revealed itself in his hobby. Ironically, the man who spent his days hunched over a desk as a minor clerk held the post of Secretary to the Dickens Society of Liverpool. 'I am considered to be quite an authority, John', he told his brother-in-law.[76] On the death of his brother George in 1910 he returned to Sligo to take a place in the family business, living alone in lodgings in the town for the six years left him. He was a man of simple tastes with few wants and, though liked by everyone, had few close friends. During his last days in a nursing home in Bray he asked Lily to get him some postcards. She asked if she should buy a half-dozen. He said no: 'he would not know what to do with more than three.'[77]

When his brother John died of pneumonia in 1900, Alfred was surprised to find himself 'sorry'. The event was so unexpected that he had not had time to summon up the Pollexfen defenses and so was disturbed by his reaction. 'It worried him. He spoke of it several times as a thing to be apologized for.'[78]

31

Lily's assessment of his life, written just before he died, may be of interest to those who like to trace the sources of her brother's poetry:

I think his life, pinched as it mostly was, has not been an unhappy one. He got happiness out of it, out of doing the same thing every day at the same time, and such little things made a not unhappy whole for him, and then the last six years have been a sort of harvest. He had money and was no longer one of a great army of no-bodies in Liverpool but had become again 'Mr. Alfred' in a place where he was know[n] and which had known and respected his people before him.[79]

And JBY, who held Alfred in deep affection for his humour and kindliness and the depth of his nature, wrote of him to Willie in 1908, after calling him 'a mental simpleton,' '*I feel that he has got something greater than either of us.*'[80]

John Anthony Pollexfen (1845 - 1900), the brother whose death filled Alfred with such embarrassing sorrow, and who appears in William Butler Yeats's poetic tribute to Alfred as 'the sailor John', shared the magnetism and primitivism of his family. He was a sailor all his life. When he was a young boatswain the captain of his ship fell mortally ill and in his extremity dismissed all the officers, all the stylish young men, 'sons of rich Liverpool merchants,' who were standing by eager to pay attendance on him, and sent for John instead, who stayed with him until he died. John told JBY the story and expressed surprise, as the captain had paid no attention to him earlier and indeed had never spoken to him, until he called for him at the end. 'The primitive in the captain recognized it in John', wrote JBY.[81] He was a good talker, and in some of his stories about life at sea he unwittingly provided John Butler Yeats with the germs of the theory that thinking was a 'consulting together of the various instincts, etc., that constitute [the] personality', a theory he felt was important enough to be passed on to his son. John Pollexfen once said to JBY that 'it was always a trouble that he must have time to think — that thinking was never a connected process. . . . If there was logic at all it came afterward. He first "made up his mind" and then expressed it perhaps by means of logic.'[82] The enforced society of a life at sea also made him the most genial and companionable of his family.[83]

William Middleton Pollexfen (1847 - 1913) was the second of the name in his generation, the first having died at the age of two a year before the younger was born. Little is known of him except he grew to adulthood, became an engineer, 'designed the quays at Sligo and produced a pamphlet explaining his unsinkable wooden ship.'[84] Then he went mad, had to be put away 'when quite young',[85] and lingered in a mental institution in Northampton, England, until his death at sixty-six in 1913.[86] His father left £2,500 for his care.[87] His mother told Lily it was her 'one great sorrow'. She 'never forgot him for an hour even', wrote Lily. 'Reports came regularly to Grandpapa from the doctors. He never opened the letter but passed it to Grandmama, who went away to read it alone.'[88] One niece insists William's illness was physical in origin, the result of a fall on the Sligo docks in which he hurt his head. But there is no record of such a fall, and his mother and father never regarded the affliction as anything other than what it seemed to be. Poor William, Lily wrote to her father, led the life 'of a caged and wingless bird', and she dreamed of a white sea bird when he died.[89]

The strain of depressive melancholia was marked in the Pollexfen family and JBY often alluded to it.[90] When his own children were growing up he saw signs of it in them and feared it might strike one or more of them beyond redemption, though it is clear that his own worry, and his children's consciousness of it, exaggerated in their own minds an unwarranted fear, as the pattern of emotional distress in the Yeatses never ranged beyond the limits found in the average family. JBY often worried about Lily, but it was Lollie who cracked under the strains of her life and showed the classic symptoms of persecution complex, mania, and depression from about 1910 until 1915. Her condition never became worse than that of what we call today a 'mild nervous breakdown'.[91] William Butler Yeats himself was often concerned that he might be a victim of depression, but if any beasts lurked in the distance his unremittent hard work and 'sense of style' kept them at bay.[92]

It was a touchy subject among the Pollexfens. William's affliction and incarceration were kept quiet, and Lily seems to be one of the few of her generation who knew all the details. Almost everyone in the next generation was unaware of the identity of the family skeleton. When Willie sent Lily a draft of his autobiography in 1915 which included an account of the psychosis of another member of the Pollexfen family — not William — Lily objected to its publication. He defended its inclusion with some spirit, noting that he had disguised the sex, omitted the tell-tale symptoms, and placed

34

the events ten years too early, so the Pollexfens could not possibly be offended. 'It might be a Yeats, for instance', he argued triumphantly.[93] Lily refused to accept his reasoning. 'I still think the incident ought to be left out', she wrote sharply, and continued, 'I think it would give pain. The Pollexfens are not very tender of the feelings of others, and any of them might point it out to [the Pollexfen involved].' Furthermore, she added in a crushing rejoinder to his last point, 'They know our Yeats relations to be all sane.'[94] WBY, showing as always great respect for his sister's judgment, omitted the doubtful passage.

There were other depressives in the Pollexfen family (and a couple of manics as well) but only two besides William reached a condition that required special care. One became morbidly depressed after the deaths of William and Elizabeth Pollexfen, who died within six weeks of each other in the autumn of 1892, and quietly but insistently discussed their deaths with anyone who came into the kitchen, even the delivery boy. A term in an institution was found necessary before recovery could be effected. Another suffered from 'a series of severe emotional breakdowns' through a long life and spent time in an asylum. Some might argue that the environment, with its absence of parental demonstrativeness and the presence of other tensions, was wholly responsible, but it may be that part of the tendency was congenital.[95]

Of the daughters in the family JBY thought Agnes (1855 - 1926) the 'most gifted and generous', one who 'really had a big brain.'[96] She was the opposite of her sister Susan, JBY's wife, with 'a faculty for fluent action and thought. . . . I think

35

she had a deeper insight in matters of feeling than any of the others but would seldom let you see what she thought.'[97] He had called her 'that termagant Agnes'[98] when he complained to his wife in 1872 about the treatment of Willie by his aunts, but in later years he came to value her qualities. 'She had the nervous and cerebral energy the others lack,' he wrote, 'and she also had that mysterious energy which I cannot describe, but which is the pulse of universal life.'[99] When he last saw her, in his studio in Stephen's Green, he impulsively kissed her and 'she trembled all over' with surprise and emotion.[100] When JBY left Ireland for New York she sent him a card of good wishes —'the only one I got from anybody,' he told WBY — and thereafter was the only one who regularly remembered him on 'occasions and anniversaries'.[101] She married Robert Gorman of Sligo and lived there all her life.

Of her older sisters Elizabeth (1843 - 1933) and Isabella (1849 - 1938), the first was a primitive in the classic Pollexfen mould, the second an artist of talent and an occultist. As a child Elizabeth could not learn the multiplication tables, and the family despaired until a teacher was hired who set them to music, after which she learned them instantly.[102] But she was caught up in the family's passion for proper marriages, although her own worked out well. When she was betrothed JBY was amused to observe that the family of her husband, the Reverend Barrington Orr, 'frankly stated that more money should be given because Elizabeth belonged to a family who were not gentlefolk.' His own family, having made a fortune manufacturing soda-water, believed itself perched on the summit of gentility. JBY recounted to Lily how surprised Barrington was to discover later that his wife was 'always quite admirable among ladies'. JBY sprang to the defence of her family, and particularly of Elizabeth Pollexfen the elder, in whom he found the pattern of her daughters:

Long ago I used to comment that the Pollexfens are not gentlemen, but that they are aristocrats. . . . When the 'genteel' ladies would after their fashion give themselves airs, I would say to myself, 'Yes, you are very nice persons and have the right ideas on many trivial though not unimportant matters. Yet Mrs. Pollexfen is a marchioness or a countess or an early daughter and a "lady" by right divine, and your daughters are only de jure.'[103]

Isabella was more complex. An artistic girl, quiet and pretty, she travelled to London during the seventies to visit her sister Susan Yeats and met her brother-in-law's friends. Among them was Oliver Madox Brown, the pre-Raphaelite painter who died young. He was attracted to Isabella and wanted to go to Sligo to meet her family. But he was dissuaded by John Butler Yeats on the grounds, probably correct, that her family would not understand him or approve of him.[104] Later she married another artist, John Varley, a painter in a family of painters only now beginning to be properly appreciated by the critics of art. Unlike some other members of the family she had, JBY thought, intelligence. 'She is somebody and you cannot easily set her aside.' He believed she had a passion to rule but no opportunity to exercise it. Instead she filled up 'the vacuum of her days by studying occult philosophy,' in which her powerful imagination was a great help.[105]

By 1878 the youngest of the Pollexfen children, Alice

(1857 - 1932), had reached her majority, and in the following year Jack Yeats, aged eight, began his long stay of eight years, the most impressionable of his life, with his grandparents in Sligo. He was their 'white-haired boy', according to Lily, 'the only one who ever had talk with Grandpapa.'[106] Jack did well enough in school, but his grandparents made no demands upon him. He fished and watched the horses and soaked up the sights and sounds of Sligo that became virtually the sole subject matter of his painting. He was like an only child of doting, elderly parents who had never had the opportunity to spoil an offspring of their youth. When he rejoined his family on their second long sojourn in London, the grandparents sold Merville and, after a short stay at Charlemont, a big yellow house overlooking the harbour, moved to a smaller place called Rathedmond, where they lived until their deaths in 1892. In 1882 William Middleton had died, and the firm of Middleton and Pollexfen became W. & G. T. Pollexfen Co., named for Grandfather William and Uncle George, who came into the firm on his uncle's death and who lived in a house, Thornhill, across the road from Rathedmond. For the next ten years the firm slipped badly, for neither George nor any of the Pollexfens was good at business.[107]

George (1839 - 1910) and his brother Fredrick, who was the black sheep, were the two sons who with their sisters Alice and Agnes lived for a long period in the Sligo area and whose lives most affected those of the Yeats children. Fredrick (1852 - 1929) had been his father's favourite.[108] But he was talkative and excitable and somewhat irrational and insistent, and the other members of the family, even the mild and in-

38

offensive Alfred, disliked him. 'He was tiresome and aggravating,' a niece of his recalls, 'and was really the only one in the family who annoyed people.'[109] He ran through money on yachts and horses and other more directly pleasurable objects, and on gambling. In 1882 Fred married a young lady from County Cavan who bore him nine children. Her trials with Fredrick drew upon her the sympathies of the rest of the family. When some years later she left him, no one held it against her. William Pollexfen cut him and his children out of his will on the ground that Fredrick had already more than consumed his share of the family fortune. At the reorganization of the Pollexfen company after William's death in 1892, Fred was excluded, and Arthur Jackson, an ambitious young man from Belfast who had married Alice Pollexfen, was brought in to rescue the firm. Fred and a friend were started up as coal merchants in Limerick, but the enterprise failed.[110] By the time he won a divorce in 1901, two of his four daughters had already been living in JBY's household for some years. They continued to live with the Yeatses until after their marriages, Lily and Lollie acting as substitute mothers. None of their aunts or uncles would help them and JBY, living in the same household, was furious.[111] He was particularly incensed at Alice Jackson who he thought had more of the world's goods than any of her brothers or sisters but guarded every florin jealously. George Pollexfen at length came to the rescue, somewhat reluctantly. When Fred's eldest daughter was married it was her cousin William Butler Yeats who gave her away. (He was 'admirable' at the job, wrote JBY to his brother Isaac. 'He has a natural instinct for pomp and ceremony, and

39

his theatrical career must have strengthened and informed it.')[112] Frederick was not invited to the wedding and reacted by sending two nasty telegrams to the bride and groom, which Lily intercepted and destroyed.[113] In the invitations and newspaper announcements the errant mother was not even acknowledged as having existence, although she lived until 1928.

During all these years Uncle George was a solid rock, often more literally than metaphorically. He had no special capacity for making money. When Arthur Jackson came into the firm he found that George had lost nearly £40,000.[114] George agreed to let Arthur run the company, put his own affairs into the hands of a worker named Doyle, whom he had saved from drink, and limited himself to acting as a kind of foreman.[115] He devoted his spare time to horses — while in Ballina he had himself raced under the name of Paul Hamilton and was admired as a jockey[116]— and astrology. He was proud of his skill in casting horoscopes. Given the birthday of York Powell, the Regius Professor of History at Oxford, but with no further identification, he correctly forecast Powell's death the following year, though Powell was in his early 50's and in perfect health when the prediction was made.[117] He was equally accurate with a new-born child.[118] A third spectacular success, a precise analysis of the actress Mary Walker (Maire nic Shiubhlaigh), was somewhat clouded by her later admission that she had given the wrong date of birth.[119]

It was during one of his nephew Willie's visits in the early 1890's that the poet and the mystic developed the strong friendship that lasted until George's death. George had been close to Willie's cousin, Lucy Middleton, who herself had

visions, especially pre-visions that WBY classed as 'verifi-
able,'[120] and Lucy and Willie spoke often of visions and magic.
During one long visit when Uncle George was ill of an infec-
tion caused by vaccination, his nephew cast images for him
and he recovered overnight. He was convinced that Willie's
mystical symbols had brought the cure, and thereafter their
friendship was solid. Yet he remained the difficult egoist that
Willie's father had known in the Isle of Man forty years
earlier. 'He never treated me quite as a grown man,' WBY
complained, 'and had the selfishness of an old bachelor.— I
remember still with a little resentment that if there was but
one kidney with the bacon at breakfast he always took it
without apology.'[121]

After George's cure they spent long periods together discus-
sing horses and occultism and staring into a crystal ball.
Occasionally George served as first audience for his nephew's
poetry,[122] and for many years he gave Willie an allowance of
a pound a week, until the mock funeral of the British Empire,
unprotested by WBY and Maud Gonne, angered him, a strong
Unionist, and he stopped the allowance.[123]

The same lack of social grace that scarred his image with
the masters at Atholl Academy continued until his death, but
he was loved by those who sought him out. York Powell
found him unbelievably fascinating.[124] Never expecting anything of anyone, George was never disappointed. He neither
liked nor disliked but took the world as it came. His actions
were based on principle, so it was always easy for him to
make a decision. Sentiment played no rôle, though occasionally simple selfishness did. He liked Lily's company and agreed

41

to help her with the education of Fredrick's children, not because he thought it was morally right but because it stopped her nagging. People whom he did not care for, or who bothered him, or expected from him what he did not care to give, he disregarded. He had a repugnance to people who were financially irresponsible: after his sister Susan died in 1900 he gradually ceased writing to his old school-friend John Butler Yeats, who could not understand George any more than George could understand him. In 1909 JBY wrote from his shabby boarding-house in New York a pathetic letter to Willie, who was selling original manuscripts to John Quinn so that he could pay his father's bills:

If he [George] knew what enjoyment meant and had some knowledge of life and the art of life, he would write to me and say, 'Old friend of my school days who married my sister and attached himself to my family and to me — would you like a hundred pounds, because if so here it is at your service.'[125]

But in his heart he must have known George would do nothing of the kind. As a young man George had had a love affair ('not, I think, very passionate', his nephew wrote of it),[126] and that and his single sea-voyage were the only unusual things that had ever happened to him. He had developed a routine in his daily life that prevented the need for decisions and so was free to worry about his health, for he was a hypochondriac, and his comfort.[127] He never lost control of himself or of the situation in which he found himself. In him JBY saw intensified what he saw in all the Pollexfens, 'the

42

awesome helplessness of ultimate human nature'. He contrived in his imagination a murder for which George was sentenced to death and wrote to his son about George's response:

On the morning of his execution he would have been the only calm person present. The turnkey, whom he would have noticed just as he did the chair he sat upon and no further, would have been in tears, and the hardened executioner would have lost some of his nerve. Yet [George] would have been calm, and when 'called' he would have risen and dressed himself a little more carefully than usual, mainly that he might be better composed and distract his thoughts. . . . Through all the trial and imprisonment nothing more articulate than a moan would have escaped from George's lips — no philosophy of life and death and no aggressive vindictiveness — and since he was by nature without any capacity for sympathy he would not have appealed to anyone. No relief in sight, he would have looked for none. That's what I mean by the awesome helplessness of human nature.[128]

George had always kept himself in the best of condition, but when Lily went to spend her vacation with him in the late summer of 1910 she found him dying of an abdominal growth. For six weeks he hung on, reading, saying little, turning his face to the wall; Lily thought he 'might just die of low spirits'.[129] 'Some people', her father wrote to Lollie, 'die very quickly,— nervous people do. But all the Pollexfens die slowly, like an Empire.'[130] In a room upstairs Lily found neatly arranged the objects that symbolized his life. There were

43

his racing jacket and cap. All about in the room are pictures and photographs of race horses and yearlings, and then the interests of his later years, books on astrology, symbolism and such. His masonic orders all are there — and all in perfect order.[131]

He died at 5.30 a.m. on September 26, 1910. Twenty-four hours earlier Lily had heard the banshee wail. It was like the cry of an old woman and was heard by the night nurse too.[132]

His funeral was splendid and brought about the last great gathering of the clan. Lily sat with Aunt Alice and two of the Jackson girls. Aunt Elizabeth Orr came to Sligo for her first visit in seventeen years.[133] In the pews ahead of them sat the men, Uncle Charles and Alfred and Arthur Jackson, Willie and Jack, the two sons of Agnes Gorman, the son of Elizabeth Orr, John Pollexfen's son Adrian, the Middleton cousins, the office staff, and the Masons. At the cemetery there were 2,000 people. 'Such a funeral', wrote Lily to her father, 'was, they say, never seen in Sligo before.'[134]

It was not a pauper's funeral. George may not have known how to make money but he knew how to keep it. The accounting of his estate showed that, from Arthur Jackson's shrewd management of the business, he had accumulated £50,000.[135] But his will was a crushing disappointment to JBY, who thought George might at least be moved by sentiment to reward the Yeatses, who were so much closer to him than the Pollexfens. Instead, with great caution and conservatism George divided his legacies into nine equal shares, one share going to each of his brothers and sisters (excepting William, still hopelessly ill in Northampton) or their heirs. He imposed

44

some special conditions, providing that the Yeats sisters were to share two-thirds of their mother's portion, the brothers one-third. To his brother Fredrick he left one-half of his ninth share in trust, the income to go to Fredrick until his death, with his children as ultimate beneficiaries. The other half he left outright to Fredrick's children.[136] To John Butler Yeats, his old school friend, alone in New York and existing only by virtue of his son's difficult generosity, he did not leave a farthing.

JBY railed at George, writing Willie that the moment he saw the will his fascination with George had come to an end. Now he saw George for what he really was, 'that Colossus the Pharisee, the moldy, old ancient Pharisee'.[137] To have made another kind of will — reducing the legacy to the 'rich sisters' and adding it to the Yeats portion was his own recommendation —[138] would have required 'affection', and George had never allowed that human quality to intervene in his decisions.[139] Principle seized and destroyed him. JBY saw him as one who succeeded in becoming no more than 'a specialist in his own life'.[140]

Fredrick screamed with rage when he read the terms of the will and threatened to contest it on the grounds that George had no right to treat a brother so unequally. Accordingly a friendly suit had to be instituted in order, as Lily Yeats expressed it, 'to put the snuffer' on Fred.[141] Jack Yeats allowed himself to become defendant in an action instituted by Arthur Jackson, the executor, and a sympathetic judge allowed Jackson's request for an order to carry out the terms of the will. Fred was granted no more than permission 'to attend inquiry in chambers at his own expense.'[142]

45

That diversion having failed, Fred now sought to become legal guardian of the two daughters who had been raised under Lily's roof for more than ten years and so gain some control of their legacies. The anguish aroused in the Yeats household can be measured by the many letters on the subject, especially those of Lily to her father as she kept him informed of developments. But with the solid and respectable Arthur Jackson on her side plus the fact — although that good Dubliner Jonathan Swift would have called it her greatest handicap in court — that she was morally in the right, Fred's manoeuvring got him nowhere, and so he became more infuriated than ever. His exclusion from his daughter's wedding angered him further. When the mad William died in 1913 Fredrick 'jumped into things again', distribution of William's estate was delayed for years, and the sum given to the Yeats children was only slightly more than half what it should have been, the rest having 'vanished on law'.[143] But that was Fred's parting shot. After it he had nowhere to go and drifted angrily through the world until his death in 1929.

Fredrick was the last of the Pollexfen sons to die. When his sister Isabella Varley died in 1938 she brought to an end a generation that had lasted just one hundred years: Charles, the first son, had been christened on the day of Queen Victoria's coronation in 1838.[144] Isabella's death marked the end of another era too, for she was the last of the Sligo Pollexfens. The names Sligo and Pollexfen will be linked together as long as poetry and art endure, yet their direct association lasted a comparatively short time in the town's history. William Pollexfen was for half a century one of the

46

most prominent men in the business affairs of the town and fathered one of its largest families. Yet by the time his last child died there was not a Pollexfen left in the county, and today only two of his descendants, who bear another surname, still live there. The Pollexfens rose suddenly in the Sligo sky, flashed across it like a comet, and disappeared. Or, to adapt a well-known ornithological simile, they came like waxwings and like waxwings went. Today the only Pollexfen entry in the Irish Telephone Directory is for W. & G. T. Pollexfen Company, Limited, and even that great firm has passed out of the control of the family.

Of all the Pollexfens, of course, the one of most interest to us is Susan (1841 - 1900), mother of the four Yeats children.[145] WBY tells us remarkably little of her in his *Autobiographies*, and students have not had much factual material to work with. At the time of the pioneer studies in W. B. Yeats's life there were surviving children of hers and it would perhaps not have been kind to speak fully of a life that had been, to put it frankly, so unhappy. Like all her sisters except Agnes, she was quiet, gentle, and sweet, and milder in some ways, as she never seemed to stand up for herself.[146] Her sisters had all married satisfactorily by Pollexfen standards and were not put to the trials that oppressed her. Susan married an Irish landlord and barrister who betrayed her family's expectations and hers, although it must be said in her husband's defense that he had not planned when he married her to abandon

47

respectability and turn Bohemian. Nor did he plan to lose his Kildare inheritance. Yet both events happened, and both unquestionably exercised a powerful effect on Susan. When he left Dublin for London in 1867, she joined him unwillingly with her young son and daughter. As a barrister's wife in Dublin she would have been assured a conventional life, a relatively secure income — even if some years might have to pass before he could achieve it — and easy access to the wild coasts of Ireland which she loved. Of course a wealthy painter in London might have made a satisfactory husband too, but it soon became clear that JBY was not to be financially successful, and the effect on his wife was catastrophic. She worried about money constantly, and she had no talent for keeping a home. 'Susan could not have boiled an egg', JBY wrote to Isaac. 'I never left home without wondering what would happen in my absence.'[147]

Yet nothing could deflect him from his course, neither his wife's complaints nor the subtle and sometimes not so subtle persuasions of his mother and his wife's father and mother. The man whom Edward Dowden thought a genius[148] and John Todhunter called 'the only man I ever really worshipped'[149] slid faster and faster toward ineffectual poverty. Yet if his wife hated the life he loved it. Todhunter visited JBY in London at his Fitzroy Road home and wrote Dowden: 'The man lives in a whirlwind of ideas. It is like breathing pure oxygen after the CO_2 of Dublin.'[150] JBY came under the spell of Edwin Ellis, many years his junior, a confident young man somewhat deficient in human understanding. 'I don't wonder at all at poor little Mrs. Yeats's hatred of him', Todhunter

48

wrote Dowden. 'He has not only estranged her husband from her, but he quietly ignores her existence.'[151]

Those first years in London, which saw the births of Lollie, Robert, and Jack, were trying ones, and the tensions are reflected in the correspondence. When Todhunter told JBY he was contemplating marriage his friend warned him that it would be 'a fatal mistake' and that he would 'repent it here-after in sackcloth and ashes'.[152] When these words were written Willie was just over four years old, Lily three, Lollie one, Bobbie was on the way and Jack was yet to come.

Susan returned to her parents with the children whenever she could, and for a while the marriage tottered. For a long time she would not recognize her husband's new career. When she registered Lollie's birth in April 1868 she listed the father's profession as 'Barrister'. But two years later she had given in, and, in registering Robert's birth, described him as 'Artist'. Her family was more stubborn. In 1873 Bobbie died suddenly of croup in Sligo while his father was painting portraits at Muckross Abbey. William Middleton Pollexfen, not yet mad, was given the job of registering the death and described the child's father as 'Barrister'. There is no question where the Pollexfen preference lay.[153]

The conflict was total and irreconcilable. 'The wearing anxiety of the last few years has told on us both,' JBY wrote Susan in 1872, 'injuring our characters as our physical strength.'[154] But he refused to abandon his career and she to accept it.

For a long time Susan showed iron determination. She refused to take any interest in his work and in all her life

49

never set foot in his studio.[155] Once JBY casually invited the Edward Dowdens to visit him in London, for he thought Dowden in Dublin was 'slowly but surely sinking into the sleep of death and that nothing but instant emigration from Ireland' could save him.[156] Susan slyly wrote Mrs. Dowden asking whether she and Edward might contribute the 'nominal' sum of fifteen shillings toward the cost of hospitality when they came. When a perplexed Dowden wrote JBY about Susan's suggestion JBY apologized in embarrassment, said such a sum was not 'nominal', that it should never have been requested, and in any case would not be accepted.[157] Dowden, a man of the greatest tact and sympathy, disempaled himself from these horns by postponing his visit to London indefinitely.

And it must have been Susan who arranged the meeting of her parents with the Dowdens in Dublin, and who persuaded her mother-in-law to write JBY offering to surrender the £50 a year he granted her as soon as his younger brother could assume the burden of her support.[158] It was apparently at Susan's insistence too that the family returned to Ireland in 1881, although JBY acquiesced as he was alarmed by her health. They settled at Howth,[159] where she was happy among the fishermen and their wives, whose doings she knew of more intimately than even the servants did. There she was able to reinforce in her children her own passionate attachment to nature, which her roots in Sligo had given her.

By 1883 the family had left Howth for less expensive lodgings in Terenure, then as now one of the least attractive sections of Dublin. JBY's hopes for success as a painter in

Dublin had not been realised and, believing that it was not his skill as an artist but the contempt bred of familiarity, which has always been so much a characteristic of Ireland's principal city, that was holding him back, he longed to return to London. There was an urgency in his desire, as his Kildare properties were about to be sold to his tenants under the Ashbourne Act and he was worried that the sum allowed him by the Land Commission might not exceed the total of his mortgaged indebtedness. In London, he thought, lay his only hope, but the family's return there in 1887 cracked Susan's spirit. Though of a strong constitution, 'her nervous system was easily upset'.[160] That winter, while the family was living at Eardley Crescent, Earls Court, she suffered a stroke. She and Lily went to her sister Elizabeth Orr at Denby, near Huddersfield, for the rest of the season. It was cold, there was snow on the ground for four months, and no one came to visit. One day, when Lily was at Huddersfield, Susan suffered a second, slighter stroke and fell down a staircase. On her return to London she found that the family fortunes had not improved. On some days there was not enough money in the house to buy food. Once Willie had to borrow three shillings from Todhunter, who with his wife had been invited to tea, and with the loan slipped around the corner to purchase the tea and bread for the unsuspecting guests.[161] Then bad news came from the Land Commission: although the purchase price fixed for the lands was enough to cover the mortgages, there was little left over, and that was placed in the controlled funds of the Commission. Further income from that source could not be counted upon.

Under these blows —'No Pollexfen could ever stand trouble', William Pollexfen's aunts had once told his wife[162]— Susan slowly but steadily deteriorated. At first she was able to be among people and would not allow herself to be described as an invalid.[163] But more and more she kept to her room. In her last years she was 'in possession of only half her mind'.[164] She died on 3 January, 1900, after an illness of more than twelve years. The weekly newspaper of St. Michael and All Angels, Bedford Park, lists the date of her death but offers no obituary.[165] She was almost a non-person for the last decade of her life.

Considering her hopes and needs, one finds it hard to wish that Susan Pollexfen Yeats had lived longer. Shortly before she died the last installment of her share of her father's legacy was paid to JBY. Thereafter no further unearned funds were available. Between 1900 and 1908 the remaining members of the family struggled to achieve solvency, not always success-fully — except Jack, of course, who had married a woman with an independent income and had struck out on his own. Willie wrote poetry and articles, Lily did embroidery, and Lollie became a printer. But JBY could not contribute his share. By the end of 1907 he was in debt to a number of Dublin creditors with no prospect of improving his circum-stances. When Lily visited America in December of 1907 to exhibit goods at the Irish Industrial Exhibition in New York he went with her, but then refused to return. For the next fourteen years until his death in 1922 he remained in New York, always hoping, but always in vain, to become a financially successful painter. His son William Butler bore

52

the financial burden of his support and John Quinn, the New York lawyer, part of the emotional burden.[166] All attempts to get him to return failed, as his stubbornness defeated sons, daughters and friends alike. 'He was headstrong,' said his daughter Lily, who worshipped him, 'and no manager'.[167]

Susan's children published little about her. WBY mentions her only occasionally in his *Autobiographies*, where she appears as a housewife mending clothes or as a storyteller talking about Sligo. 'I can see now that she had great depth of feeling,' her son writes, 'that she was her father's daughter. My memory of what she was like in those days has grown very dim, but I think her sense of personality, her desire of any life of her own, had disappeared in her care for us and in much anxiety about money.'[168] In the letters written during the last decade of her life he seldom mentions her except as an invalid who is doing better or worse on a particular day.

Lily supported her father's charge that she was 'not at all good at housekeeping or child-minding'. And she goes further : 'She was prim and austere, suffered all in silence. She asked no sympathy and gave none. . . . When we were children and were ill she always said, "Grin and bear it", and so she did. She endured and made no moan.'[169] And although JBY was careful in speaking to his children never to say a word against his wife, and indeed spoke with the warmest feeling about her all his life, a year before he died he wrote to Willie, 'I often said to your mother that her affection was a matter that one *inferred*. No one ever saw it or heard it speak.'[170]

She remained a Pollexfen to the end, frightened of affection yet deeply needing it, loving the simple fisher-folk of the simple country and unable to accept the sophisticated intellectuals of the big city.[171] But she could not escape from the false gods of her family. Twelve years after her death JBY could write to his daughter, 'Had I had money your mother would never have been ill and would be alive now — that is the thought always with me — *and I would have done anything to get it for her* — but had not the art.'[172] Anything, that is, except become a practical man, as indeed he could not.

It is now a commonplace of Yeatsian criticism that without a knowledge of the poet's life much of his poetry cannot be fully appreciated. And surely we cannot understand WBY fully unless we know the Pollexfens, as we cannot understand the art of Jack Yeats without knowing Sligo. Was Willie in truth a Yeats? JBY thought Uncle George would have been happy if only his favourite nephew, who shared so many of his own qualities, had been named Pollexfen instead.[173]

We do not know enough about the workings of genes and chromosomes. Every human being is a bewildering combination of his ancestors, the immediate remembered and the past unknown. Against the claims of individuality we have all seen at times how a child, like Shakespeare's fox, no matter how tame, how 'cherish'd and lock'd up, will have a wild trick of his ancestors'. A husband finds the source of his children's weaknesses in the imperfect protoplasm of his wife's family. When Willie responded sharply to a letter from Lollie about her troubles with Miss Gleeson of the Dun Emer Guild his father wrote him in exasperation, '*Why do you write such offensive letters?* There is nothing fine in a haughty and arrogant temper. It is Fred Pollexfen's characteristic. . . . You treat Lollie as if she was dirt.'[174] But he knew brother and sister were much alike, and both Pollexfens: 'Like Lollie he is not always easy to live with,' he told Isaac, 'having her tendency to melancholy, and like her when the fit is on him he does not in the least mind how he wounds your feelings. In this way they are both like their poor mother.'[175] The testimony to WBY's haughtiness and apparent snobbishness is abundant and indeed almost universal; but placed among the Pollexfens he seems perfectly ordinary. The seriousness, earnestness, and thoroughness of his art are pure Pollexfen. His tendency towards the mystic and the occult — he received messages from George Pollexfen years after his uncle had died[176]— is easily understood as a strain of the Pollexfen heritage, shared with George and with Isabella Varley, and with his sister Lily, who saw prophetic visions of extraordinary accuracy. So with other members of the family. Jack, a man of the greatest humour himself, claimed there was no such thing as comic writing and proved impervious to the works of Benchley, Thurber, and the Grossmiths.[177] The troubles of William Pollexfen the younger find an unhappy, if fortunately not perfect, counterpart in the crisis in Lollie's life between 1910 and 1915.

The Yeatses may have been 'The Good People,' as JBY told his son, but he added that although they were loved they were not feared, and so passed 'making no mark'.[178] They 'are doomed,' he wrote to his brother Isaac, 'to be like water spilled on the ground.'[179] But some instinct for immortality worked deep in John Butler Yeats, and perhaps that was what led him to thicken the Yeats blood with that of the Pollexfens, that family of 'brooding imagination,' of a 'native, an indestructible and wholly unconscious spontaneity'.[180]

'I have hoped,' he told Isaac, 'that by some good chance one of [the Yeatses] might marry and meet thereby with the right kind of mate, so that the Yeats essence or elixir shall be saved and not spilled on the ground.' And he concludes with a quiet satisfaction which the world has endorsed: 'I think I myself mated well when I married with the Pollexfens. You yourself can see that in my daughters and sons.'[181]

1 Mrs. John Butler Yeats (Susan Mary Pollexfen), ca. 1867. This drawing dates from the period of that reproduced on the cover.

2 Enniscrone, County Sligo, 1866. A drawing made during a family holiday. Lily was born here on August 25th.

3 Enniscrone, County Sligo, 1866. A companion drawing to number 2.

4 W. B. Yeats as a baby, 1866.

5 W. B. Yeats as a boy, ca. 1876.

6 Elizabeth Corbet (Lollie) Yeats, 3 June 1877.

7 Susan Mary (Lily) Yeats, 1877.

8 W. B. Yeats, 1886. A similar sketch appears as the frontispiece to *Mosada*.

9 W. B. Yeats, ca. 1887.

10 W. B. Yeats, June 1889.

11 Lily Yeats, May 1889.

12 W. B. Yeats, 8 December 1897.

13 Self Portrait of the artist, John Butler Yeats, 1905.

The drawing on the cover is of Mrs. John Butler Yeats.

1   Mrs. John Butler Yeats (Susan Mary Pollexfen), ca. 1867.

2   Enniscrone, County Sligo, 1866.

3   Enniscrone, County Sligo, 1866.

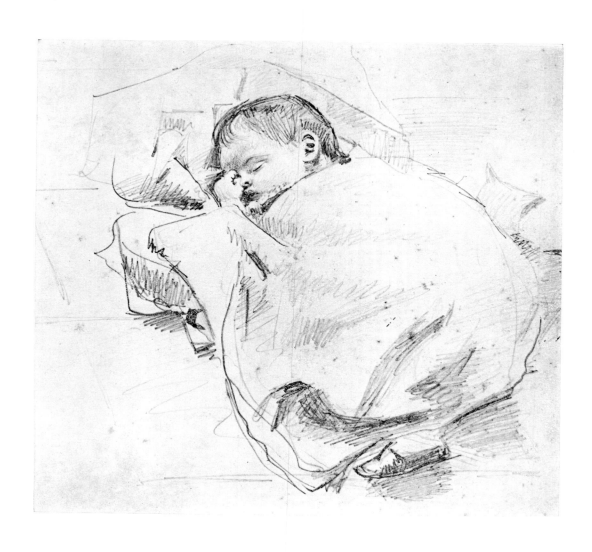

4   W. B. Yeats as a baby, 1866.

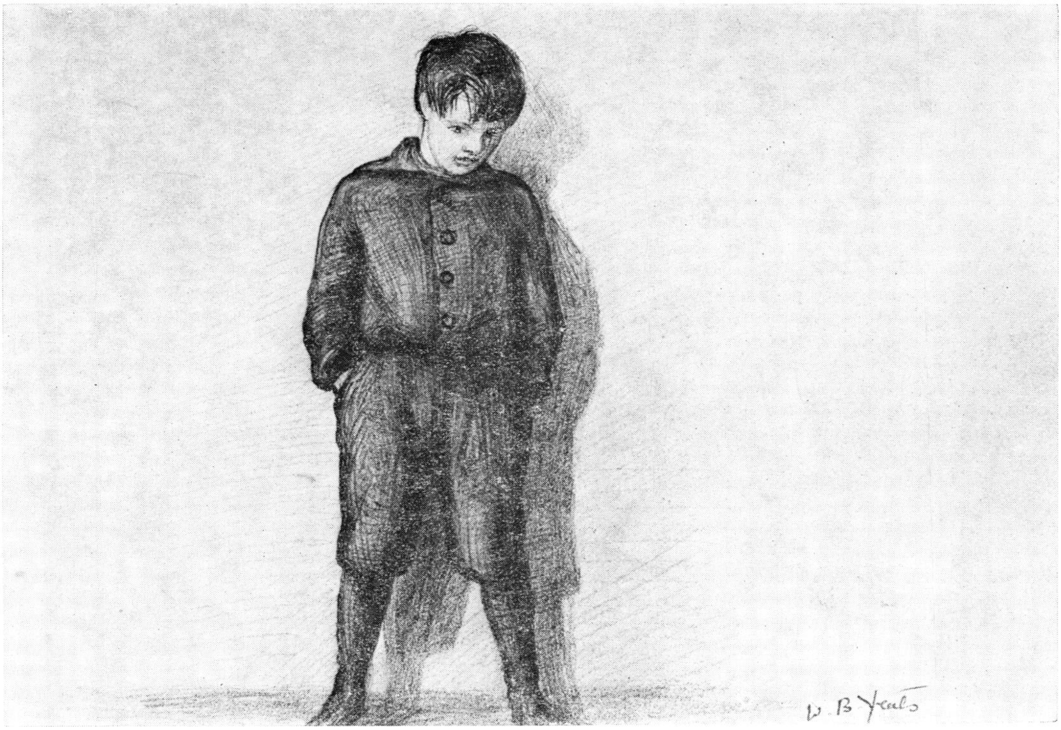
W. B. Yeats

5 W. B. Yeats as a boy, ca. 1876

6   Elizabeth Corbet (Lollie) Yeats, 3 June 1877.

7 Susan Mary (Lily) Yeats, 1877.

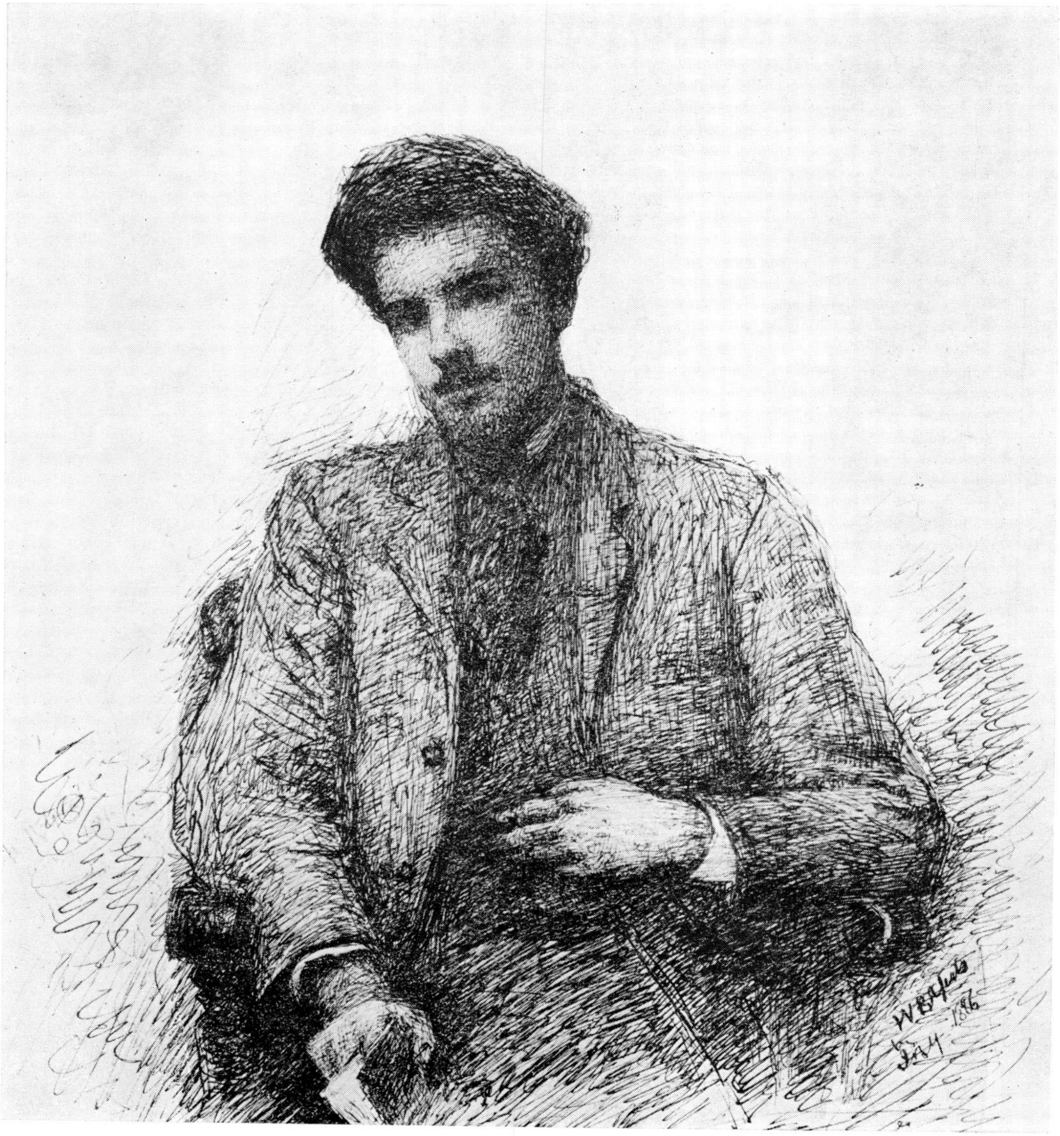

8 W. B. Yeats, 1886.

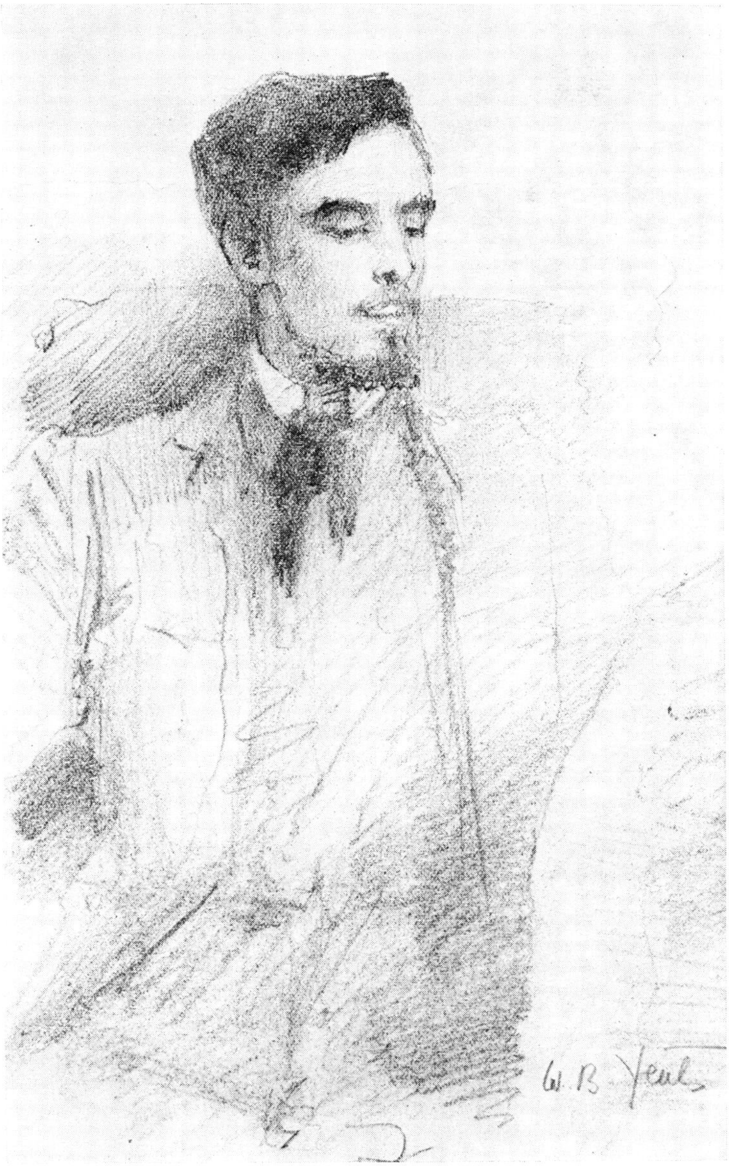
W. B. Yeats

9 W. B. Yeats, ca. 1887.

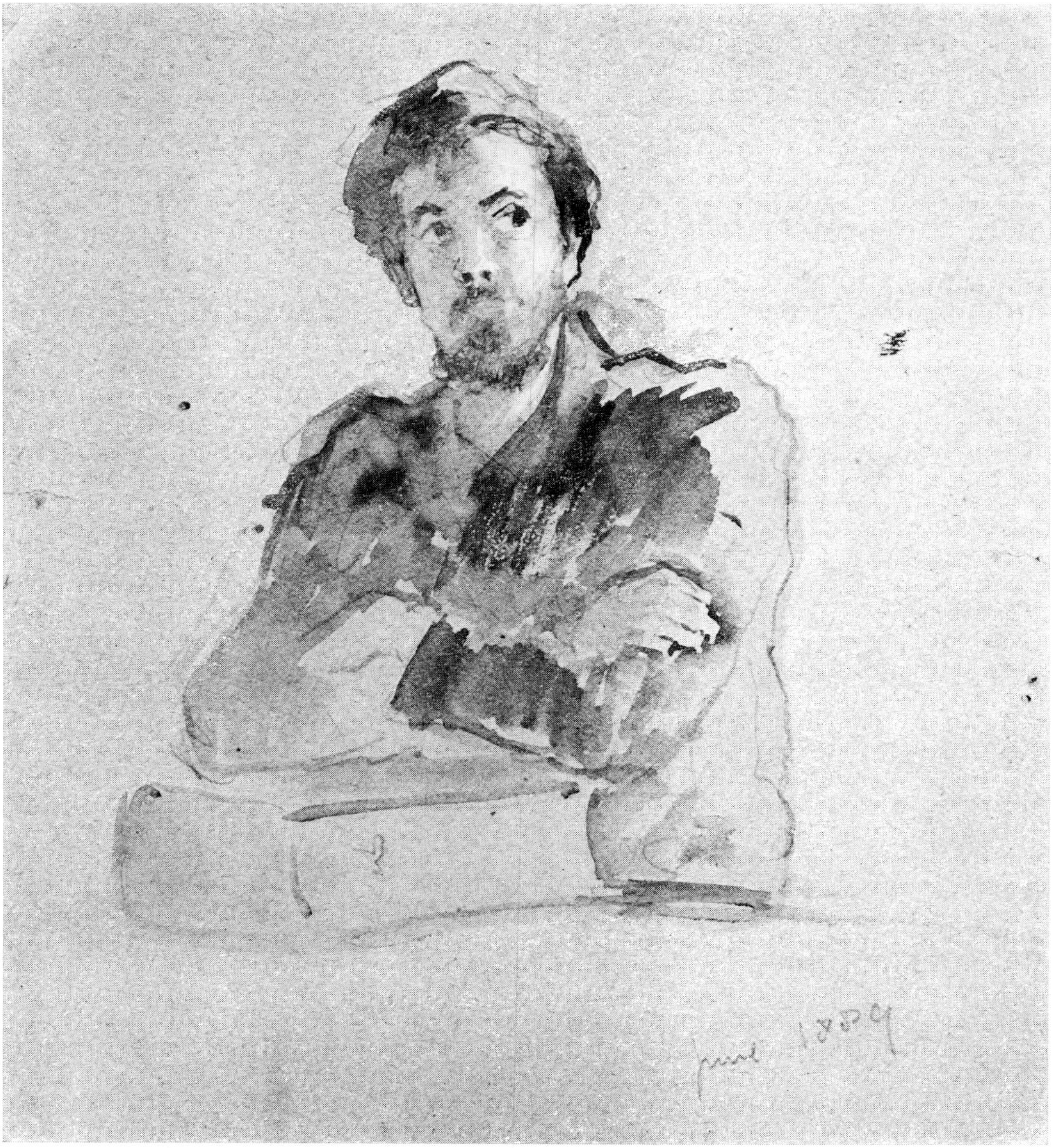
June 1889

10 W. B. Yeats, June 1889.

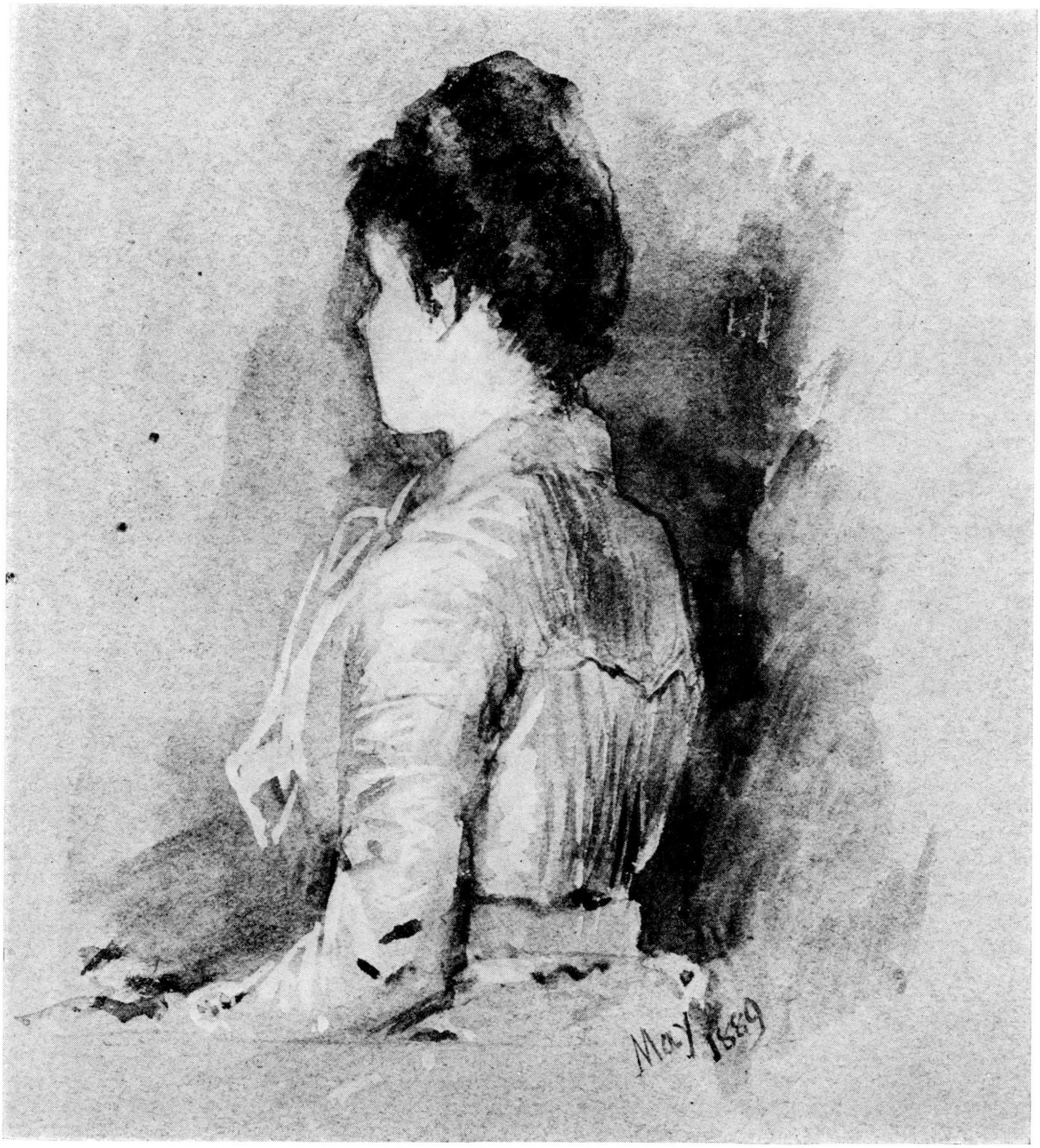
May 1889

11 Lily Yeats, May 1889.

12   W. B. Yeats, 8 December 1897.

13   Self Portrait of the artist, John Butler Yeats, 1905.

GENEALOGY OF THE POLLEXFENS AND YEATSES

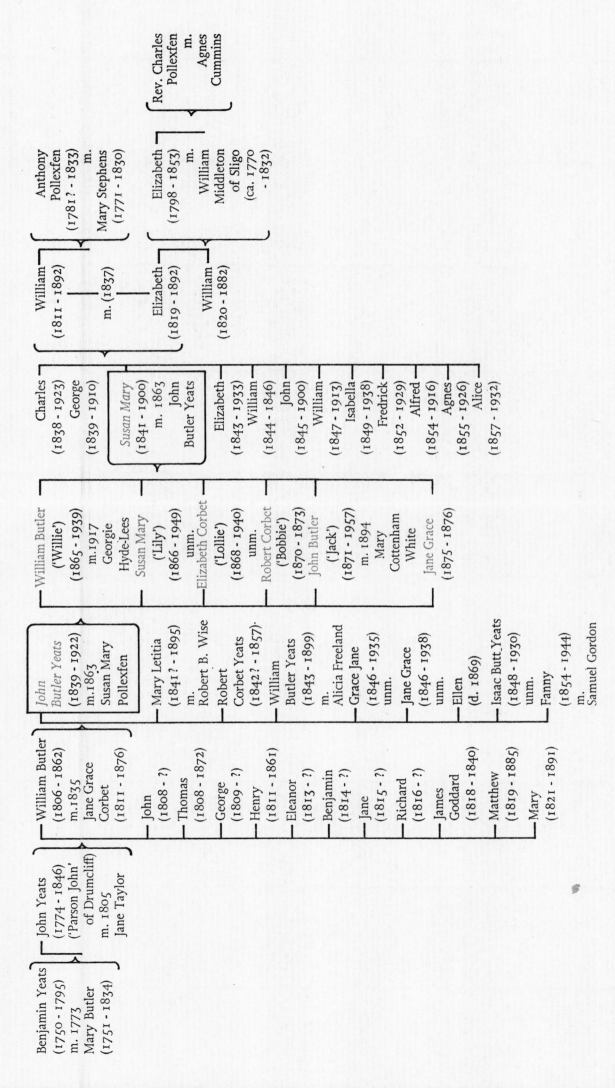

GENEALOGY OF THE POLLEXFENS AND YEATSES

ACKNOWLEDGEMENTS AND REFERENCES

This paper is an expanded version of a talk entitled 'The Pollexfens' delivered at the Yeats International Summer School in Sligo on 15 August, 1968; I thank Dr. T. R. Henn, Director of the School, for the opportunity to appear there. Many people have shared with me their knowledge of Sligo and the Pollexfens: Mrs. Sheelah Kirby, Mrs. Ida Varley Dewar-Durie, Mr. Edward Fawcett Brown, Mr. Robert W. Brown, Dr. Oliver Edwards, and Mr. J. M. Keohane. I have also received help from Miss Olive Purser, Mrs. Andrew Jameson, Beatrice Lady Glenavy, Mrs. Lennox Robinson, the late Bishop T. Arnold Harvey, the late Dr. Thomas MacGreevy, Mr. C. P. Curran, the Rev. W. J. Jenner, Mr. Leonard Elton, Mrs. Michael B. Yeats, Miss Frances-Jane French, Miss Stella Mew, Miss Hilary Pyle, Mr. Terence De Vere White, Mr. Padraic Colum, Miss Nora Niland of the Sligo County Museum, Mr. James Provost of the Dublin Records Office, and Mrs. Bridget MacMenamin and Mr. Charles Thomas of the Kings Inn Libraries in Dublin.

A Fellowship of the American Council of Learned Societies, a grant from the American Philosophical Society, and several Ford Foundation-Union College Faculty Research grants have provided me with the time and other facilities needed for research into the life of John Butler Yeats. The present essay will reappear in modified form in a biography of John Butler Yeats now in preparation.

The staff at the library of Trinity College Dublin has been most helpful: I am particularly indebted to Mr. William

O'Sullivan, Mrs. Maired Looby, Miss Maria Kenny, Mr. Frank Byrne, and Mr. William Dieneman. Members of the staff of Shaffer Library, Union College, have also been kind and generous in their assistance: I thank Dr. Edwin K. Tolan, Miss Ruth Anne Evans, Mrs. Loretta Walker, the late Mr. Charles Wilde, Mr. Edward Elliot, Mr. Wayne Somers, and Mr. Leonard Halperin. I appreciate the opportunity to have worked in the National Library of Ireland in Dublin and the British Museum in London. Mr. K. R. Mason, Shipping Editor of Lloyd's, Mr. Kenneth McGuffie of the Admiralty Registry, and Miss Daphne A. Pipe of the National Maritime Museum have provided important information. Efficient secretarial and stenographic work has been provided by Mrs. Dora Pugh, Mrs. Audrey Werner, Mrs. Georgia MacFarlane, Mrs. Lillian Heinen, Mrs. Susan Thomas, Miss Patricia Stoddart, Mrs. Joanna Fotheringham, Mrs. Barbara Seeger, Mrs. Elizabeth De Feo and Mrs. Hilda Clohesy. I am particularly grateful to the late Mrs. Elizabeth T. Wilsey and regret that she could not live to see the results of her labours in print.

Valuable suggestions about the text have been offered by Dr. T. R. Henn, Prof. A. N. Jeffares, Dr. Oliver Edwards, Mrs. Daphne Fullwood, Mr. John Kelly, and Mrs. Jocelyn Harvey, but of course none of them is responsible for errors of any kind.

For aid equally valuable if less direct I thank Dr. Carl Niemeyer, Dr. Neal W. Allen, Jr., and Dr. Theodore D. Lockwood. Professors Donald Torchiana and Glenn O'Malley shared with me their typescripts of the letters of John Butler Yeats to many of his American friends. Mr. Richard Hirsch contributed countless hours in putting hundreds of letters in proper order and providing an index for them.

Almost all the facts in the essay come from unpublished material in the possession of Miss Anne Butler Yeats and Senator Michael Butler Yeats, and to them my gratitude is beyond measure. Without their generosity, cooperation, and sympathy the paper could not have been written.

Finally, I owe a debt which cannot properly be described to my wife, Harriet D. Murphy, who has given hundreds of hours of her time to labour both profound and menial which has contributed greatly to the making of this work.

Unpublished material is noted in the references in the following manner: a single name and date will indicate a letter *from* John Butler Yeats to the person named (e.g. 'Lily 1910 June 25' indicates a letter from JBY *to* his daughter Lily); a pair of names is always self-explanatory (e.g., 'WBY to Lily 1915 Jan 11'): undated letters are identified by their opening words (e.g., WBY, *n.d.*, 'This is why I said . . .'). When reference is to a letter consulted in a published version I give the source in parentheses after the description of the letter; otherwise the original letter is implied. 'WBY' is William Butler Yeats, 'Lily' is Susan Mary Yeats (JBY's daughter), 'Lollie' Elizabeth Corbet Yeats, 'Jack' John Butler Yeats, Jr. (Jack Yeats), and 'Isaac' Isaac Butt Yeats. I have regularized the spelling of 'Lily' and 'Lollie' to conform to their own preferences. Other unpublished material is described as follows:

[John Butler Yeats's manuscript memoirs, in three volumes, pages unnumbered]: Memoirs (followed by volume and folio number.)

[Lily Yeats's Family Scrapbook, containing essays, photographs, newspaper clippings, genealogical tables, etc.]: Lily Yeats's Scrapbook (followed by subtitle in quotation marks where applicable, e.g., 'Elizabeth Pollexfen').

[Notebook by Lily Yeats entitled by her 'Odds and Ends']: Odds and Ends (followed by subtitle where applicable).

[Lily Yeats's Diary]: Lily Yeats's Diary, year, month, and day.

[Lollie Yeats's Diary]: Lollie Yeats's Diary, year, month, and day. [Extracts from the diary have been published in Hone, Joseph, *J. B. Yeats: Letters to His Son W. B. Yeats and Others* (New York: E. P. Dutton, 1946), pp. 291 - 298, and in J. Hone, 'A Scattered Fair,' *The Wind and the Rain*, vol. iii, No. 3, Autumn 1946].

Legal documents and records are listed in a way that will most clearly identify them.

A single proper name standing alone indicates that the person named supplied the information in personal conversation.

Four published works have been abbreviated in the references:

Early Memories: Yeats, John Butler, *Early Memories; Some Chapters of Autobiography* (Churchtown, Dundrum: The Cuala Press, 1923).

WBY, *Autobiographies*: Yeats, W. B., *Autobiographies* (London: Macmillan, 1966).

Hone, *J. B. Yeats, Letters*: Hone, Joseph, *ed.*, *J. B. Yeats: Letters to His Son W. B. Yeats and Others, 1869 - 1922* (New York: Dutton, 1946).

Wade, *Letters*: Wade, Allan, *The Letters of W. B. Yeats* (London: Rupert Hart-Davis, 1954).

The standard works alluded to, in addition to those above, are:

Hone, Joseph, *W. B. Yeats, 1865 - 1939* (London: Macmillan, 1965).

Jeffares, A. Norman, *W. B. Yeats, Man and Poet* (London: Routledge and Kegan Paul Ltd., 1962).

Ellmann, Richard, *Yeats, The Man and the Masks* (London: Faber and Faber, 1965).

Both Hone and Jeffares were given access to some of the unpublished material that provides the basis for this essay, which supplements and expands upon what they have written. All students of Yeats owe an enormous debt of gratitude to these and other early workers in the field.

1   Lily 1916 Sept 15.
2   Lily 1917 Oct 10.
3   WBY 1909 Mar 24.
4   Edward Dowden 1884 Jan 8.
5   Isaac 1911 Apr 28. Cf. Lollie 1911 Apr 14: 'In you are two races, the Yeats and the Pollexfen. The first always makes the best of things, and the second makes the worst of things. The first wd impel you to like your fellow creatures and live in gay harmony with them. The other impels you to dislike them and get into discomfortable relations with them.'
6   Lily 1916 Sept 15. Part of the letter is published in Hone, *J. B. Yeats Letters*, p. 229, but the punch line is omitted.
7   John Butler Yeats (1839-1922); William Butler Yeats (1843-1899); Robert Corbet Yeats, of whom I know only that he 'died at 15 at Sandymount Castle' (Lily Yeats's Scrapbook): his dates were approximately 1842-1857. A fourth brother, Isaac Butt Yeats (1848-1930) was too young to attend school with the others.
8   'Striping', an Anglo-Irish term, meant dividing land into strips or plots [see *New English Dictionary*, IX, 1146: 'stripe', definition sb. 3, 6b]. A local historian writes that two land agents, Barber and Yeats, were chiefly responsible for the striping, which the tenants thought 'unwarranted and unfair' [O'Rorke, Rev. T. F., *History of Sligo: Town and County* (Dublin: James Duffy, n.d.), I, 485]. In his account book of the Kildare property of his nephew John Butler Yeats, Matthew Yeats reveals himself as a most unsympathetic and unpleasant person with no understanding of the problems of the native Irish people.
9   Thomas Yeats's abandoning of his career so struck Sir William Wilde, father of Oscar, that whenever he saw JBY he said, 'Fancy Tom Yeats buried in Sligo' (WBY 1916, Sept 6). JBY repeats Wilde's remark about a dozen times throughout his correspondence; see, *e.g.*, Hone, *J. B. Yeats Letters*, p. 79.
10 Lily Yeats's Scrapbook, 'Our Grandmother Elizabeth Pollexfen—born Middleton.'
11 O'Rorke, *History of Sligo*, II, 330-331.
12 *Early Memories*, p. 12.
13 WBY 1916 Sept 20.
14 Memoirs, I, f. [10].
15 *Early Memories*, p. 12.
16 p. 13.
17 *Early Memories*, p. 13. I have changed the book's reading of 'irresponsiveness,' which may be a misreading of JBY's difficult handwriting.
18 Memoirs, I, f. [16]. A characteristic embellished misquotation of Wordsworth's *Excursion*, I, 80.

19 *Early Memories*, pp. 13, 16, 17, 18.
20 WBY 1921 Feb 4.
21 WBY 1916 Sept 20.
22 Lily Yeats's Scrapbook, 'Our Grandmother Elizabeth Pollexfen — born Middleton'; Yeats, W. B., *Autobiographies*, p. 69. Lily says he went to Portugal, WBY that he went to Spain; I give him the benefit of both accounts. Lily misspells the name of the ship as 'Baccaloo.'
23 Memoirs, III, f. [53].
24 *Early Memories*, p. 85.
25 Lily Yeats's Scrapbook, 'Mama's Health and Other Things.'
26 Susan Pollexfen 1863 Apr 20.
27 The acreage is taken from documents in the Dublin Records Office, and is Irish measure. It corresponds to about 560 acres English or American measure
28 WBY 1918 Feb 10.
29 *Ibid*.
30 Lily 1912 Oct 30, and in many other letters.
31 Memoirs, I, f. [62].
32 To the observation about the Pollexfen facility for remembering newspaper verses JBY added, 'My son inherited this ear for rhyme.'
33 Edward Dowden 1884 Jan 8. This is apparently the earliest use by JBY of the metaphor of the sea-cliffs. Years later he was to record: 'One day while still a school boy he [WBY] showed me some verses that delighted because of a wild and strange music. I remembered his mother's family and their puritan grimness and, turning to a friend, said, ' "If the sea-cliffs had a tongue what a wild babbling there would be! I have given a tongue to the sea-cliffs." ' (Memoirs, I, f. [62]). But the phrase 'I have given a tongue,' etc. does not appear in the letter to Dowden.
34 Memoirs, I, f. [26]. The National Gallery of Ireland owns one of these sketches, No 2675, 'James Whiteside, Lord Chief Justice, 1804-1876.' It is dated February, 1866.
35 Personal conversation.
36 For the specific, identifiable influences of JBY on William Butler Yeats, see the excellent account by Jeffares, A. N., 'John Butler Yeats', *In Excited Reverie* (New York: Macmillan, 1965), pp. 24-47.
37 See WBY, n.d., 'It is the easiest . . .' [1904], (also published in Hone, *J. B. Yeats Letters*, No. 40, pp. 79-80): 'I would not write so freely on this subject [i.e., the Yeatses] but that you have never met any of my family . . . .' Matthew the Land Agent was the only one of JBY's uncles Willie knew, and he was infected by 'that worst of all heresies against humanity, the heresy of Bible Christianity.'
38 Lily Yeats's Scrapbook, 'Our Grandmother Elizabeth Pollexfen — born Middleton.'
39 Lily Yeats's Scrapbook, 'Lily and May Morris.'

40   See Harper, George M., ' "Go Back to Where You Belong": Yeats and the Theme of Exile.' Professor Harper's paper, a model of creative scholarship, was read at the Yeats International Summer School in Sligo on August 16, 1968.

41   W. B. Yeats, *Autobiographies*, p. 9.

42   Lily Yeats's Scrapbook, 'Grandfather William Pollexfen.'

43   Lily Yeats, Odds and Ends, 'The Big Noise.'

44   Lily Yeats's Scrapbook, 'Grandmother Yeats.'

45   Lily Yeats's Scrapbook, 'Grandfather William Pollexfen.'

46   Information about the Pollexfens and Middletons generally is taken from Lily Yeats's Scrapbook and from Odds and Ends.

47   O'Rorke, *History of Sligo*, I, 486.

48   Lily Yeats's Scrapbook, 'Our Grandmother Elizabeth Pollexfen — born Middleton.'

49   WBY 1914 June 13.

50   WBY 1916 Sept 18 (second letter of this date, beginning 'Why am I writing . . .').

51   Jeffares, A. N., *W. B. Yeats, Man and Poet* (London: Routledge & Kegan Paul, Ltd., 1962), p. 14.

52   WBY 1915 July 30.

53   WBY 1909 Mar 5.

54   Lily 1910 June 25.

55   Isaac 1916 Apr 3.

56   Memoirs [miscellaneous fragment in typescript, p. 17].

57   See introductory paragraph to these references.

58   Lily 1922 Feb 1. This was the last letter, and one of the best, written by JBY. He visited the doctor immediately after finishing it; two days later he was dead.

59   See Murphy, William M., 'Father and Son: The Early Education of William Butler Yeats,' *A Review of English Literature* (London: Longmans), October, 1967, Vol. VIII, No. 4, pp. 75-96.

60   W. B. Yeats, *Autobiographies*, p. 10.

61   See pp. 34-35 *infra*.

62   Lily 1910 Nov 6. See also Lily 1922 Feb 1: 'Fred would have been a good man if his parents had taken a little interest in him, but there was no one to advise him except his brother Charles, and Charles was never a good influence at any time. I once told George that I thought Charles had been Fred's ruin, and it annoyed George very much *because he knew it was true*. Charles was the bad influence in the family. I saw that from the first.' Earlier in the letter he had written: 'A parental solicitude is not among the Pollexfen traits.'

63   Susan Pollexfen 1862 Nov 29.

64   WBY 1906 Aug 3.

65   *Ibid*.

66   WBY 1921 Feb 4.

67   WBY 1916 Sept 6.

68 Edward Fawcett Brown.

69 W. B. Yeats, *Autobiographies*, p. 10.

70 WBY 1916 Apr 20.

71 WBY, *n.d.*, 'This is why I said . . .'

72 Lily to JBY 1916 Sept 19.

73 WBY 1919 Feb 12.

74 WBY, *n.d.*, 'This is why I said . . . .'

75 Lily 1916 Aug 30.

76 *Ibid*.

77 Lily to JBY 1916 July 13

78 WBY 1915 Apr 25.

79 Lily to JBY 1916 Aug 14. Lily sent WBY a letter, now lost, in which she repeated this paragraph and apparently wrote even more about Alfred and the Pollexfens, for WBY's response included the first draft of his ode to Alfred with an acknowledgment that it was merely an expansion of her letter. His letter and draft are in the National Library of Ireland, MS. 3255. See Murphy, William M., ' "In Memory of Alfred Pollexfen": W. B. Yeats and the Theme of Family,' *Irish University Review*, Vol. I, No. 1, Autumn, 1970, pp. 30-47.

80 WBY 1908 Aug 11. The passage is quoted in Hone, Joseph, *W. B. Yeats, 1865-1939* (London: Macmillan, 1965), p. 16.

81 WBY 1916 Sept 18, No. 2 ('Why am I writing . . .').

82 WBY 1916 Apr 28. Printed in Hone, *J. B. Yeats Letters*, No. 163, p. 224.

83 Jack 1916 May 31. John Pollexfen visited the Yeatses in London whenever he could, both at Fitzroy Road in the seventies and Bedford Park in the nineties. JBY drew more pencil sketches of him than of any other Pollexfen save Susan Yeats. Lily Yeats in her diary (1895 Aug 13) records John's concern when calling at Bedford Park at a time when he had just come from his home in Liverpool, where the children were afflicted with mumps. He refused to enter until assured that the Yeatses were not afraid of the illness.

84 W. B. Yeats, *Autobiographies*, p. 10.

85 Lily Yeats's Scrapbook, 'Our Grandmother Elizabeth Pollexfen — born Middleton.'

86 For details about the date and place of his death I am indebted to Dr. Oliver Edwards.

87 A copy of his will is in possession of Senator Michael B. Yeats.

88 Lily Yeats's Scrapbook, 'Our Grandmother Elizabeth Pollexfen — born Middleton.'

89 Lily to JBY 1913 July 9.

90 Cf. for example Isaac 1912 July 10: 'Lily never speaks of it to anyone, and to me always speaks of it as nerves, as I to her — but it is depressive mania, and it affected more or less most of the Pollexfens. Three of them were in Asylums.'

91 Those who remember Lollie testify to her compulsive talking and her fussing with little things. 'A non-stop talker,' the late Dr. Thomas MacGreevy called her. I am indebted also to Mrs. Michael B. Yeats, who studied painting under her when a girl, Dr. Oliver Edwards, and Mr. Leonard Elton, for their recollections of her.

92 Cf. WBY's *A Journal 1908-1914* (unpublished), Item 44, 1909, undated (between January 31 and February 3): 'I begin to wonder whether I have and always have had some nervous weakness inherited from my mother. (I have noticed my own form of excitability in my sister Lolly, exaggerated in her by fits of prolonged gloom). ... In Paris I felt that if the strain were but a little more I would hit the woman who irritated me, and I often have long periods during which Irish things — it is always Irish things and people that vex, slight follies enough — made life nearly unendurable. The feeling is always the same: a consciousness of energy, of certainty, and of transforming power stopped by a wall, by something one must either submit to or rage against helplessly. It often alarms me; is it the root of madness?'

'... I should learn to exclude this irritation from my conversation, at any rate, as certainly as I have learned to exclude it from my writings and my formal speech. In one way it has helped me, for the knowledge of it has forced me to make my writings sweet-tempered and, I think, gracious. There was a time when they were threatened by it; I had to subdue a kind of Jacobin rage. I escaped from it all as a writer by my sense of style....'

From his Unpublished Autobiography, Section VI: 'It was only during my recent years that, though I am working very steadily, more than two hours original composition ['does not' *obviously omitted*] bring me almost to nervous breakdown. In almost all the members of my family there is some nervous weakness.'

In the summer of 1933 WBY wrote to John H. Pollock, who published a brief biography of him in 1935, that he had to give up 'all the writing I could through some sort of nervous breakdown.' (*Daily Telegraph*, 1967 Oct 27).

93 WBY to Lily 1915 Jan 11.

94 Lily to WBY 1915 Jan 12.

95 Could the troublesome gene have come from old William Pollexfen? To Lily's descriptions of his alternately silent and explosive irritability may be added two interesting passages from letters of JBY to his brother Isaac:

1911 June 30: 'A great doctor here, Dr. Spitzka, says mind and digestion are closely connected. He has cured several cases of insanity of *long standing*, simply by attending to their digestion — and his remedies for digestion *are very drastic* .... It was by treating his digestion that old Wm. Pollexfen was cured. Stokes and all the great Doctors said that Wm. Pollexfen needed rest and so he took rest, months of it, and was no better. Then a *little* doctor, and an enthusiast somewhere in England,

and an Irishman to boot, said he must live regular hours and dine never later than 1 o'clock, and after months of this he was cured.'

[1911] Dec 12: 'Lollie is an abiding anxiety. Long ago I several times was most anxious about her — she is so constantly unhappy, too like "Grandpapa." '

96   Isaac 1911 Aug 5.
97   WBY 1916 Sept 20.
98   Susan Pollexfen Yeats 1872 Nov 1.
99   WBY 1908 Aug 11.
100 Isaac 1912 Jul 12; WBY 1916 Sept 20.
101 WBY 1908 Aug 11; Isaac 1910 Oct 22.
102 WBY 1915 Sept 6 (first letter of this date, 'I am writing . . .').
103 Lily 1910 June 25.
104 Hone, *J. B. Yeats Letters*, pp. 48-49.
105 WBY 1916 Sept 21.
106 Lily Yeats's Scrapbook, 'Grandfather William Pollexfen.'
107 Andrew Jameson, the distiller, charged that George Pollexfen had no head for business (JBY to WBY [1904?], n. d., 'It is the easiest . . .' [Printed in Hone, *J. B. Yeats Letters*, No. 40, p. 80]). After William Middleton's death the Pollexfen prosperity faded ('Money was not so plentiful,' says Lily of the years after 1887 [Scrapbook, 'Our Grandmother Elizabeth Pollexfen — born Middleton.']). It is significant that a son-in-law, Arthur Jackson, rather than a Pollexfen son, was called upon to run the business. The earlier spectacular success of the Pollexfen interests may perhaps be laid at the door of William Middleton or of a particularly fortunate local business monopoly, quite unintended, at the right time. Wondering about George's will shortly after his death JBY wrote to Lollie (1910 Sept 30): 'He possibly will think it his duty to leave a good deal to Arthur Jackson, since Arthur has really *made* the money by his energy and enterprise, George being rather a *saver* of money than a *maker* of it.'
108 Lily 1915 June 23.
109 Mrs. Ida Dewar-Durie.
110 Mr. Edward Fawcett Brown.
111 WBY [1904?], n.d., 'It is the easiest . . . .' 'I was thinking about the callous way in which the Pollexfens are leaving those four little girls all to their fate. Alice Pollexfen, who is exceedingly well off, does not care a half-penny what becomes of them. It is the way with people engaged in trade, and particularly if they have raised themselves by trade . . . . They are engaged in a hard fight, and people who have raised themselves or who intend to raise themselves always drop their poor relations.' (Hone prints part of the letter [No.40, pp. 79-80] in *J. B. Yeats Letters* but omits this passage).
112 Isaac 1911 Aug 5.
113 *Ibid.*
114 WBY to Lady Gregory [1910 Sept 29] (Wade, *Letters*, p. 553).

115 Lily 1922 Feb 1; WBY to Lady Gregory [1910 Sept 28] (Wade, *Letters*, p. 552).

116 Lily Yeats's Scrapbook, 'Our Grandmother Elizabeth Pollexfen — born Middleton.' Cf. Hone, *W. B. Yeats, 1865-1939*, p. 16.

117 *Early Memories*, p. 96. George Moore alludes to George Pollexfen as 'a celebrated occultist whose predictions were always fulfilled.' *(Ave* [New York: Boni and Liveright, 1923], p. 24).

118 WBY to Lily [1895 Jan 20] (Wade, *Letters*, p. 245).

119 WBY 1921 Apr 29.

120 Unpublished Autobiography, Section XXVI.

121 *Ibid.*

122 WBY to Katharine Tynan [1888 after Sept 6] (Wade, *Letters*, p. 87).

123 Mr. Edward Fawcett Brown.

124 *Early Memories*, p. 93.

125 WBY 1909 Mar 5. Cf. Lollie 1909 Nov 25: 'If George Pollexfen knew how to obtain for himself a little real enjoyment he would take a great surprise out of me and himself also by writing a cheque in my favour for £50 or £100.'

126 W. B. Yeats, *Autobiographies*, p.69.

127 When Lily left Sligo suddenly, where she had been visiting George, she saw he was depressed and attributed his condition to her departure; but he assured her it was only the damp weather (Lily Yeats's Diary, 1895 Oct 7).

128 WBY 1915 July 30.

129 Lily to JBY 1910 Aug 22.

130 Lollie 1910 Sept 30.

131 Lily to JBY 1910 Sept 20.

132 Lily to JBY 1910 Sept 29.

133 Lily to JBY 1910 Sept 5.

134 Lily to JBY 1910 Sept 29.

135 WBY to Lady Gregory [1910 Sept 29] (Wade, *Letters*, p. 553).

136 Notes in Lily Yeats's Scrapbook.

137 WBY 1916 Sept 6.

138 WBY 1912 Sept 20.

139 WBY 1916 Sept 6.

140 Memoirs, I, f. [10].

141 Note in Lily Yeats's Scrapbook.

142 High Court of Justice in Ireland, Chancery Division, 1910, No. 1005; Notice of Judgment Dec. 7, 1910: Estate of George Thomas Pollexfen, between Arthur Jackson, plaintiff, and John Butler Yeats, Jr., defendant.

143 Lily to JBY 1917 Jan 23.

144 Lily Yeats, Odds and Ends, 'Susan Pollexfen.'

145 In addition to the four children who survived her, and Robert Corbet, already mentioned, she also bore Jane Grace Yeats, August 29, 1875 — June 6, 1876.

146 Mrs. Ida Dewar-Durie.

147 Isaac 1915 Dec 29.

148 Edward Dowden to Richard Garnett 1888 May 22 (Garnett, R. S., *ed.*, *Letters About Shelley* [London: Hodder and Stoughton, 1917], pp. 165-66).

149 John Todhunter to Edward Dowden 1878 Nov 22 (Trinity College Dublin Library, Dowden Correspondence, No. 196).

150 John Todhunter to Edward Dowden 1869 Sept 27 (Trinity College Dublin Library, Dowden Correspondence, No. 55).

151 John Todhunter to Edward Dowden 1870 Jan 14 (Trinity College Dublin Library, Dowden Correspondence, No. 60).

152 John Todhunter to Edward Dowden 1869 Sept 27 (Trinity College Dublin Library, Dowden Correspondence, No. 55).

153 For the birth and death records and their significance I am indebted to Dr. Oliver Edwards.

154 Susan Pollexfen Yeats, *n.d.* [1872], ('My chief anxiety . . .').

155 W. B. Yeats, *Autobiographies*, p. 62. WBY's impression that his mother took no interest in her husband's work is probably correct in a general way. But she did visit his studio and showed concern at least about the financial prospects of his work. See her letter to Matthew Yeats, *n.d.*, *ca.* 1880 ('Your letter and the draft . . .'): 'I meant to have written you this afternoon's post, but went to the Studio and forgot to take your letter . . . and . . . instead of writing at the Studio waited till I came back. We were all disappointed about the portrait not getting into the Academy.'

156 John Todhunter to Edward Dowden 1869 Sept 27 (Trinity College Dublin Library, Dowden Correspondence, No. 55).

157 Edward Dowden 1879 May 11.

158 Jane Grace Corbet Yeats to JBY [1873?] June 18. The brother was William Butler Yeats. She received £100 a year for life from her husband's estate (see Dublin Records Office, 1839, Bk. 6, No. 19), and JBY voluntarily added £50 a year out of his own means.

159 W. B. Yeats, *Autobiographies*, p. 31.

160 Lily Yeats's Scrapbook, 'Mama's Health.'

161 Lollie Yeats's Diary 1888 Sept 27.

162 WBY 1910 Dec 14. He repeats the remark in Lollie 1911 Apr 14.

163 Lily Yeats's Scrapbook, 'Mama's Health and Other Things.'

164 WBY 1915 Apr 25.

165 For showing me his copy of this newspaper I thank the Rev. W. J Jenner of St. Michael and All Angels, Bedford Park.

166 Quinn was JBY's anchor to windward during his years in New York. JBY wrote him hundreds of letters. One of these [ca. 1919 Jan, beginning 'All through the worst part of my illness. . .'] gives a detailed account of his emotional difficulties as an improvident husband and unsuccessful father (as he thought) during the 1880's and 1890's.

167 Lily Yeats to Oliver Edwards in conversation. I am grateful to Dr. Edwards for letting me know of this interesting remark.

168 W. B. Yeats, *Autobiographies*, p. 31.

169 Lily Yeats's Scrapbook, 'Mama's Health and Other Things.'

170 WBY 1921 Feb 2. Cf. also WBY 1915 Apr 25: '[With the Pollexfens] feelings, especially the affections and sympathies, were put under a ban .... There was however one feeling accepted and allowed sway — married people might like each other. Only even here there was a limitation. They must never give expression to the feeling in public or private. It was puritanism without religious ecstasy or exultation.'

171 WBY 1915 Apr 25: 'She was there as always, really disliking everybody and everything, yet accepting everybody and everything. She was never happy except in the country. She liked green countries and sky and the sea. I never knew why or how she liked them. When in Devonshire and I away in London she wrote every day and always described the state of the sea and the sky. And latterly when in possesion of only half her mind it was her daily task to write to me, and always she described the sky as seen from the parlours in Blenheim Rd — *described it well*. It was the only thing she ever wrote about, for everything else was only a worry.'
JBY was relentlessly conservative on the subject of marriage. He wrote to WBY (1916 Jan 15): 'People seem to me to have quite forgotten *what a wife is*. A man may admire one woman and be in love with another, and all sorts of wanton fancies in his restless heart may play continually about a third. There is one woman whom *he accepts and she is* his wife — all her limitations, her want of intellect, even her want of heart. All her infirmities and all her waywardness he accepts and would not have any of them altered. If there be such a woman she is his wife. The feeling grows slowly. It is not affection as it is not passion. It [is] just *husband's feeling*, and she has doubtless a corresponding *wife's feeling*.'

172 Lily 1912 Sept 20. That JBY worried about his failure to provide is vividly shown by his account of a dream that disturbed his slumber almost forty years after the event it depicts: 'I dreamed last night that I had a visit from your grandfather, who asked me how long I expected him to support me. I thought I was staying at Merville. I awoke miserable, and remained so for a long time.' (WBY 1914 May 10).

173 *Early Memories*, p. 97.

174 WBY 1906 Aug 3.

175 Isaac 1915 Dec 29. Even when no family crisis loomed, WBY could be difficult socially. In 1896 he visited his family at Bedford Park, and JBY wrote of him to Lily, who was in France as a governess: 'Willie has been staying here the last few days. Today he went back. He has the greatest wish to be friendly and peaceable, but he can't manage it, and tho' I was very sorry to see him go, for he is in good humour, both

most attractive and affectionate, still wherever he is there is a constant strain and uneasiness.'

Yet the Pollexfens didn't see things as JBY did, since Willie's success was in unproductive art rather than in the making of money. 'I used to plead for Willie,' wrote JBY to Lily (1916 Sept 15 [Hone prints a passage from the letter but omits what is quoted here]), 'by pointing out that he was like his mother. But they were scornful and would have it that he was just like his unsuccessful father, unsuccessful and therefore wicked.'

176   WBY to Lily 1915 Aug 21. ('I am sorry to hear how ill you are. Lolly has told me. I wonder if this is what George Pollexfen's ghost meant when it asked after you and Lolly and said 'ah poor Lilly.' It may have known what was coming. By the by it insisted that it would appear to me when alone and insisted that I would be able to see. I have seen nothing yet . . . ').

177   Beatrice Lady Glenavy, *Today We Will Only Gossip* (London: Constable, 1964), p. 180.

178   WBY 1909 Mar 24.

179   Isaac 1920 May 4 (second of this date: 'Willie dined here last night . . .').

180   WBY 1916 Sept 18

181   Isaac 1920 May 4 ('Willie dined here last night . . .').

Date Due

PRINTED | IN U. S. A.